Intersectional Leadership

Strategies for Building *Resilient* Workforces

Kimberlee Armstrong, Ed.D., M.B.A.

This book is dedicated to everyone who has inadvertently contributed to harm in the workplace. May it inspire us to improve and excel, as it offers a call to action to do better. I have faith in our potential to effect positive change.

"We can do hard things."
-Dr. Renard Adams

This book is devoted to Marianne Noel, Thaddeus, Dujuan, Damarcus, Charianne, Matthew, Raymond, Samiah Noel, Josiah, Kristian Mekhi, Nyalani Noel, aunties, uncles, cousins, nieces, nephews, friends, colleagues and my supporters. I am because you are. Your presence, support, and love have shaped me into the person I have become.

Thank you for being a part of my journey.

To my amazing Portland team, thank you for leading out loud. The work we are doing on behalf of an entire generation is humbling. We are #ForwardTogether!

In Service

Kimberlee Michele Armstrong

© 2023 Kimberlee Armstrong. All rights reserved.

All rights reserved. No part of this publication may be reproduced, stored in a retrieval system, or transmitted in any form or by any means, electronic, mechanical, photocopying, recording, or otherwise, without the prior written permission of the copyright holder, except in the case of brief quotations embodied in critical reviews and certain other noncommercial uses permitted by copyright law.

When forms and practice documents appearing in this work are intended for reproduction, they will be marked as such. Reproduction of their use is authorized for educational use by educators, local school sites, and/or noncommercial or nonprofit entities that have purchased the book.

For permission requests, please contact the publisher at the following address:

In Lead Out, LLC

1171 Second Ave

Chula Vista, CA 91911

info@inleadout.com

www.inleadout.com

First Edition: April 2023

ISBN: 979-8-9880482-0-6

Printed in the United States of America

This book is a work of nonfiction. While every effort has been made to ensure the accuracy and reliability of the information contained herein, neither the author nor the publisher can be held responsible for any errors, omissions, or inaccuracies. Any opinions expressed in this book are those of the author and do not necessarily reflect the views of the publisher. Readers are encouraged to verify any information presented in this book before relying on it in any way.

Reviewed by:

Dr. Anthony B. Craig, University of Washington, L4L Ed.D Program Director & Professor of Practice

Dr. James E. Crawford, Superintendent (7/2023)

Dana Geaslen, Assistant Superintendent

Dr. Justin Irish, Superintendent

LaTasha Mahar, MBA

Cassandra Waller-Mims, Business Owner

Design
Crystal Chavez

INTERSECTIONAL LEADERSHIP: BUILDING RESILIENT WORKFORCES

The Search: Equity Based Hiring   p. 12

This involves creating hiring practices that are designed to promote equity and diversity, such as blind resume review and targeted outreach to underrepresented groups.

The Invitation: Symbolic Interaction   p. 34

This framework emphasizes the importance of shared meaning and interaction in shaping individual and group behavior. In the workplace, this can involve promoting open communication and active listening, as well as creating opportunities for collaborative problem-solving.

Labels: Affinity Grouping   p. 58

Affinity grouping involves creating spaces for individuals with shared identities or experiences to come together and support each other. This can help to promote resilience in the face of discrimination and other challenges.

Leveling: Equity & Justice   p. 80

These frameworks emphasize the importance of promoting equity and justice in the workplace, and addressing the ways in which discrimination and stereotypes can impact individuals' performance and well-being.

She/Her: Feminist Framework   p. 100

This framework highlights the ways in which gender inequality and discrimination can impact the workplace. It emphasizes the importance of promoting gender equity and creating a workplace culture that is supportive of all genders.

I am: Stereotype Threat   p. 120

This refers to the impact of negative stereotypes on individual performance and well-being, and highlights the importance of creating a workplace culture that is supportive and inclusive of all employees.

Throughlines: Ecosystem of Racism   p. 142

This framework highlights the ways in which racism and other forms of discrimination can be deeply embedded in social systems and structures. It emphasizes the importance of addressing these issues at a systemic level, through policies and practices that promote equity and justice.

Investments: Cybernetics   p. 160

This framework emphasizes the importance of feedback and self-correction in creating effective systems. In the workplace, this can involve creating mechanisms for feedback and evaluation, as well as promoting continuous learning and improvement.

Future Ready: Succession Planning   p. 186

This involves developing a plan for identifying and developing the next generation of leaders within an organization. This can involve providing opportunities for training and development, as well as creating a culture of mentorship and support.

Adelante: Intersectional Leadership   p. 206

This involves promoting a leadership style that is supportive and inclusive of all employees, regardless of their background or identity.

Foreword

In today's increasingly interconnected and diverse world, cultivating a workforce that thrives on the principles of inclusion, equity, and diversity is not just an admirable goal, but a strategic imperative. Organizations that successfully embrace these values have a competitive advantage, as they are more innovative, resilient, and ultimately, better equipped to navigate the challenges and opportunities of the 21st century. It is my pleasure to introduce "Intersectional Leadership: Strategies for Building a Resilient Workforce," a timely and comprehensive guide that offers valuable insights and practical tools for fostering a culture of inclusivity and empowerment.

Dr. Kimberlee Armstrong's rich background in education and leadership, as well as her own personal journey as a first-generation college student, uniquely positions her to offer a thoughtful and informed perspective on the subject of intersectional leadership. Through her extensive experience in various roles across the educational sector, Dr. Armstrong has witnessed firsthand the transformative power of inclusive practices and policies. This book is a testament to her unwavering commitment to equity and her belief in the limitless potential of every individual.

"Intersectional Leadership" takes the reader on a journey through the various facets of diversity and inclusion, providing a solid foundation of knowledge upon which organizations can build. Dr. Armstrong's writing is both accessible and engaging, as she weaves together a tapestry of theory, research, and real-world examples that bring the concepts to life. The book is a treasure trove of actionable strategies and best practices, empowering leaders and organizations to create more inclusive workplaces where all employees can thrive.

As you delve into the pages of "Intersectional Leadership," I am confident that you will be inspired by Dr. Armstrong's vision and dedication to creating a world where every individual is valued, respected, and empowered to achieve their fullest potential. By embracing the lessons and strategies outlined in this book, leaders and organizations can not only create more inclusive and equitable workplaces but also contribute to a more just and compassionate society. It is an honor to be part of this vital journey towards creating a more resilient and inclusive future for all.

Damarcus Thomas
Data Scientist & Associate Professor

About the Author

Dr. Kimberlee Armstrong began her educational career as a public school teacher in the Puyallup School District (WA) and has since devoted over two decades to various roles in support of elementary, middle, and high schools, with a focus on leading and supporting staff. She is now the Chief Academic Officer in Portland, Oregon. Dr. Armstrong's previous roles include cabinet-level Executive Director of Equity and Public Relations in Edmonds School District (WA), Assistant Superintendent in Tamalpais Union High School District (CA), and Associate Superintendent in Santa Rosa City Schools (CA). Her leadership journey includes serving as principal at Kenmore Junior High and later at Mount Miguel High School (CA).

Dr. Armstrong earned her Bachelor of Arts Degree in Communication from California State University East Bay, Masters in Business Administration from City University of Seattle and later obtained a Doctor of Education Degree in Educational Leadership and Policy Studies with a Washington State Superintendent Certification from the University of Washington.

With a steadfast dedication to learning and liberation, Dr. Armstrong is actively involved in community service and academic enhancement. Her commitment to service is evident through her membership in Sigma Gamma Rho sorority and her leadership role in the National School Public Relations Association, where she leads a national team focused on identifying best practices and performance measures in equity and diversity communications.

As a first-generation college student who attended Abraham Lincoln High School and City College of San Francisco, Dr. Armstrong is passionate about promoting equitable advancement, nurturing a growth mindset, and developing resilient workforces for employees across the United States. Inspired by her own experiences, she is determined to create a work environment that is adaptable, supportive, and empowers individuals to thrive as their authentic selves.

"The Search"

There was a technology startup called TechTrek that was struggling to attract and hire a diverse pool of candidates. They had a reputation for being a "boys club," and many people from underrepresented communities felt that they did not have a fair shot at getting hired.

TechTrek's leadership team recognized that they needed to make changes in order to create a more inclusive hiring process. They decided to adopt an equity-based hiring approach to address systemic barriers that may be preventing diverse candidates from applying and succeeding in the hiring process.

The first step they took was to revise their job descriptions to be more inclusive and to focus on the essential skills and qualifications needed for the job. They also expanded their recruiting sources to include partnerships with diversity-focused organizations and job boards that catered to underrepresented communities.

To ensure that the selection process was fair and transparent, TechTrek implemented structured interviews and objective criteria to evaluate candidates. They also trained interviewers on unconscious bias and provided feedback to candidates to help them improve their interview skills.

As a result of these changes, TechTrek saw a significant increase in the diversity of their applicant pool, interviewees, and new hires. They also received positive feedback from candidates and employees about the fairness and transparency of the hiring process.

TechTrek's commitment to equity-based hiring did not stop at the hiring process. They also implemented diversity and inclusion training for all employees and created a culture that valued and supported all employees, regardless of their background.

Over time, TechTrek became known for its commitment to equity-based hiring and diversity and inclusion. They were able to attract and retain top talent from a wide range of backgrounds, and their organization culture became a model for others to follow.

In the end, TechTrek's success was a testament to the power of equity-based hiring to create a more diverse and inclusive workplace.

Chapter 1
Equity Based Hiring

Are you seeking to become an effective leader who empowers their team and cultivates an inclusive, diverse, and innovative work environment? Look no further than this book, your new steadfast companion. It will guide you on an odyssey of personal and professional growth, empowering you to lead people and nurture dynamic and awe-inspiring environments.

As a leader, you face complex challenges and navigate multiple relationships in your organization. This resource will help you unravel the narratives echoing across your workplace and spark curiosity-driven innovation. By embracing this journey, you can unlock your potential to lead effectively amidst the diverse intersections of people.

This book begins with the concept of equity-based hiring, a vital seed that fosters growth and cultivates a resilient workforce. The concept of equity-based hiring is rooted in the principles of equity and social justice, which have been part of various movements throughout history. In the United States, for example, a pivotal moment was the Civil Rights Act of 1964 that prohibited discrimination based on race, color, religion, sex, or national origin in employment practices, among other areas.

First, let's ground in our key term, equity. Equity refers to fairness, justice, and impartiality in the treatment of all individuals, regardless of their race, gender, ethnicity, socioeconomic status, or any other characteristic. In an equitable society, all individuals have equal access to resources, opportunities, and privileges, and are not disadvantaged by systemic or institutional biases or discrimination. The goal of equity is to create a level playing field where everyone has a fair chance to succeed, and where no one is held back or excluded due to factors beyond their control.

The concept of equity-based hiring emerged as an effort to go beyond mere compliance with anti-discrimination laws and to actively promote diversity, equity, and inclusion (DEI) in hiring practices. The idea is to create a level playing field to eliminate systemic barriers that may prevent underrepresented groups from being considered or hired.

Equity-based hiring draws on research in areas such as unconscious bias and social identity theory to develop hiring practices that build resilient workforces. This involves identifying and addressing biases and barriers in the hiring process. While the concept of equity-based hiring has been around for many years, it has gained increasing attention in recent years as leaders have become more aware of the importance of diversity and inclusion in the workplace. Leaders are now recognizing that a diverse and inclusive workforce can bring a variety of benefits, such as increased innovation, improved decision-making, and higher employee engagement and retention. As a result, many organizations are now adopting equity-based hiring practices as part of their overall diversity and inclusion strategies.

Equity-based hiring involves using inclusive language in job postings and descriptions, actively recruiting candidates from underrepresented groups, and providing training to hiring managers on how to identify and reduce unconscious biases in the hiring process.

Equity-based hiring also involves creating a work environment that is welcoming and supportive of all employees, regardless of their background or identity. This includes providing opportunities for professional development and advancement, offering flexible work arrangements, and implementing policies and practices that promote joy and resilience.

Equity-based hiring serves as a vital foundation for cultivating a robust and adaptable workforce. This approach necessitates continuous assessment and refinement of recruitment strategies, with the goal of fostering genuine diversity and inclusivity throughout the organization.

Attracting Candidates

To attract a diverse pool of candidates, organizations should use a variety of channels to communicate and advertise job openings. This can include using social media platforms such as LinkedIn, Twitter, and Facebook to advertise job openings and reach diverse populations. Organizations can use hashtags related to diversity and inclusion to help their posts gain more visibility. This is a great opportunity to make sure your diversity is reflected across your social channels.

Organizations can also partner with organizations that serve underrepresented populations, such as minority professional associations, community-based organizations, and diversity-focused job boards. These partnerships can help reach a wider pool of diverse candidates. Get comfortable having conversations about why candidates of color choose other organizations.

Attending diversity-focused career fairs and job events can also be a great opportunity to connect with diverse candidates in person. These events can be an opportunity to showcase the organization's commitment to diversity and meet potential candidates face-to-face. Think of ways you can move with intentionality, like considering letters of intent or on the spot hiring at job fairs and recruitment events.

Using job boards that cater to specific demographics, such as women, people of color, and LGBTQ+ communities, can help to reach a more targeted audience of candidates. Organizations can also optimize job descriptions for diversity and inclusion by using inclusive language that reflects your commitment to diversity and inclusion. Be authentic. Get real.

Encouraging employees to refer diverse candidates for job openings and offering incentives for successful referrals can also help to tap into the networks of diverse employees and increase the pool of diverse candidates.

By incorporating these strategies, organizations can increase the reach of their job postings and attract a more diverse pool of candidates. This will help to ensure that your organization's workforce reflects the diversity of the communities you serve and foster a culture of inclusivity.

Adjust Hiring Criteria

Organizations can adjust their hiring criteria to be more inclusive of candidates from diverse backgrounds. This can help to identify qualified candidates who may not meet traditional requirements, such as educational or work experience. To adjust hiring criteria, organizations can review and revise job descriptions to ensure that they are not unnecessarily restrictive. By focusing on essential skills and qualifications, rather than limiting requirements, organizations can attract a wider pool of highly qualified candidates.

Competency-based hiring is another approach that can help to identify candidates with transferable skills and potential for growth. There are brilliant individuals who have a lot to offer and this approach evaluates candidates based on their ability to perform specific job-related tasks, rather than relying on specific educational or work experience requirements. This can be a more inclusive approach that identifies candidates who may have valuable skills and experience that are not reflected in their formal education or work history.

Considering lived experiences, such as volunteering, personal projects, or community involvement, as a qualification for the job can also help to identify candidates with valuable skills and experience. This can be particularly beneficial for candidates from underrepresented communities who may not have had access to traditional educational or work experience opportunities.

Structured interviews that focus on specific competencies or skills required for the job can help to minimize unconscious bias and provide a more objective evaluation of candidates. Offering training and development opportunities to candidates who may not meet all of the qualifications but show potential and willingness to learn can also help to develop a more diverse and skilled workforce.

Implementing diversity-focused metrics to track the diversity of the candidate pool and evaluate the effectiveness of the revised hiring criteria can help to identify areas for improvement and measure progress towards a more inclusive hiring process. By adjusting hiring criteria to be more inclusive of candidates from diverse backgrounds, organizations can create a more diverse and skilled workforce that better reflects the communities they serve.

Evaluate Interview Process

To further action on equity-based hiring, organizations should evaluate their interview process. One way to do this is to train interviewers on unconscious biases and provide them with tools to recognize and avoid it. Providing education on different types of biases, such as affinity bias, stereotype threat, and halo effect, can help to reduce their impact on the interview process. We cover these topics in greater detail in chapter three.

Using standardized interview questions can also help to minimize the impact of interviewer bias and provide a more consistent evaluation of candidates. These questions should be relevant to the job requirements and assess candidates' skills and qualifications objectively. Additionally, using structured interview processes, which involve a set of standardized questions and a scoring rubric to evaluate candidates' responses, can provide a more objective evaluation of candidates and reduce the impact of subjective assessments.

Offering interview training and resources to candidates, such as sample questions and feedback on their performance, can help to level the playing field and provide all candidates with equal opportunities to succeed in the interview process. It's also important to solicit feedback from candidates on their interview experience, including any concerns or suggestions for improvement. This can help to identify areas for improvement in the interview process and ensure that it is inclusive and equitable.

By evaluating the interview process and implementing strategies to ensure that it is inclusive and equitable, organizations can create a fair and objective hiring process that attracts and retains a diverse pool of candidates. This can bring a variety of benefits to the organization, such as increased innovation and improved decision-making.

Monitor Hiring Metrics

To achieve equity-based hiring, organizations should regularly review their hiring metrics to track the diversity of their applicant pool, interviewees, and new hires. This can help identify areas of improvement and measure progress towards creating a diverse and inclusive workplace. Consider this as a relevant and important data point in your strategic plan, priorities, or an annual report

One strategy for monitoring hiring metrics across different stages of the hiring process, such as the applicant pool, interviewees, and new hires. This can include tracking demographic data such as gender, race, ethnicity, and age. Using data analytics to track and analyze hiring metrics can help to identify patterns and trends over time, and identify areas for improvement in the hiring process.

It's also important to regularly review hiring metrics to ensure that the organization is making progress towards equity-based hiring. By setting targets and goals for diversity and inclusion in the hiring process, and regularly evaluating progress towards these goals, organizations can ensure that they are on track to achieve their objectives.

Incorporating feedback from employees is another important strategy for creating an inclusive workplace. This can involve conducting surveys, focus groups, and other forms of employee feedback to ensure that the organization is creating an environment where all employees feel valued and supported.

By monitoring hiring metrics and tracking progress towards equity-based hiring, organizations can identify areas for improvement and create a more diverse and inclusive workplace. Creating an inclusive workplace can lead to a variety of benefits, such as increased innovation, improved decision-making, and higher employee engagement and retention.

STICKING POINT

Equity-based hiring requires ongoing evaluation and adjustment of hiring practices, which can be time-consuming and resource-intensive. Some organizations may not have the resources or support necessary to implement equity-based hiring practices effectively.

Some people may have unconscious biases that affect their perception of candidates from underrepresented groups. These biases can manifest in various forms, such as assuming that a candidate from a certain background is not qualified or has a poor work ethic. Overcoming these biases requires self-awareness and training, which can be challenging for some people.

Equity-based hiring is a complex and ongoing process that requires a commitment to change and a willingness to challenge traditional hiring practices and biases. While it can be difficult for some, it is an important step towards building a resilient workforce. To overcome the challenges of equity-based hiring, organizations must invest in resources and support for their hiring managers and teams.

THE SEARCH: EQUITY BASED HIRING

Key Questions

What is equity-based hiring?

Equity-based hiring refers to the practice of creating and implementing hiring processes that prioritize fairness, diversity, and inclusion. The goal is to ensure that all candidates have an equal opportunity to be considered for job openings, regardless of their race, ethnicity, gender, sexual orientation, age, religion, or other protected characteristics.

What are some strategies for attracting a diverse pool of candidates?

To attract a diverse pool of candidates, organizations can use a variety of channels to advertise job openings, such as social media platforms, diversity-focused job boards, and partnering with organizations that serve underrepresented populations. Organizations can also attend diversity-focused career fairs and job events and optimize job descriptions for diversity and inclusion.

How can organizations adjust their hiring criteria to be more inclusive of candidates from diverse backgrounds?

Organizations can adjust their hiring criteria by reviewing and revising job descriptions to ensure that they are inclusive and not unnecessarily restrictive. They can also consider using competency-based hiring and taking into account lived experiences. Using structured interviews and offering training and development opportunities can also help to create a more diverse and skilled workforce.

What are some strategies for evaluating the interview process to ensure that it is inclusive and equitable?

Organizations can train interviewers on unconscious biases and provide them with tools to recognize and avoid them. Using standardized interview questions, structured interview processes, and offering interview training and resources to candidates can also help. It's important to solicit feedback from candidates and regularly evaluate interview metrics to track progress towards a more inclusive and equitable interview process.

Practice 1.1

Math Movers Inc. is a large company that is committed to promoting diversity and inclusion in their hiring practices. They have identified that their workforce does not currently reflect the diversity of the communities they serve, and they are committed to changing this.

Math Movers Inc. begins by reviewing their job descriptions and making sure that they are inclusive and not unnecessarily restrictive. They focus on the essential skills and qualifications needed for each job, rather than requirements that may limit the candidate pool.

To attract a diverse pool of candidates, Math Movers Inc. uses a variety of channels to advertise job openings, including social media platforms such as LinkedIn, Twitter, and Facebook. They also partner with organizations that serve underrepresented populations, such as minority professional associations, community-based organizations, and diversity-focused job boards.

Math Movers Inc. attends diversity-focused career fairs and job events to connect with diverse candidates in person. They showcase their commitment to diversity and inclusion at these events and use them as an opportunity to network with potential candidates.

To adjust their hiring criteria to be more inclusive of candidates from diverse backgrounds, Math Movers Inc. uses competency-based hiring. They evaluate candidates based on their ability to perform specific job-related tasks, rather than relying on specific educational or work experience requirements. They also consider lived experiences, such as volunteering, personal projects, or community involvement, as a qualification for the job.

Math Movers Inc. evaluates their interview process to ensure that it is inclusive and equitable. They train interviewers on unconscious biases and provide them with tools to recognize and avoid it. They use standardized interview questions and structured interview processes that involve a set of standardized questions and a scoring rubric to evaluate candidates' responses. They offer interview training and resources to candidates, such as sample questions and feedback on their performance, to level the playing field and provide all candidates with equal opportunities to succeed in the interview process.

Math Movers Inc. regularly reviews their hiring metrics to track the diversity of their applicant pool, interviewees, and new hires. They establish baseline metrics for diversity and inclusion across different stages of the hiring process and use data analytics to track and analyze hiring metrics. They regularly review hiring metrics to ensure that they are making progress towards equity-based hiring and set targets and goals for diversity and inclusion in the hiring process. They also incorporate feedback from employees to ensure that they are creating an inclusive workplace that attracts and retains a diverse workforce.

By implementing equity-based hiring practices, Math Movers Inc. creates a more diverse and inclusive workplace that better reflects the communities they serve. They attract and retain a diverse pool of candidates, which brings a variety of benefits to the organization, such as increased innovation and improved decision-making. They also foster a culture of inclusivity, which leads to higher employee engagement and retention.

1. What specific steps did Math Movers Inc. take to promote diversity and inclusion in their hiring practices?

2. How did Math Movers Inc. adjust their hiring criteria to be more inclusive of candidates from diverse backgrounds?

3. What strategies did Math Movers Inc. use to attract a diverse pool of candidates for their job openings?

4. How did Math Movers Inc. evaluate their interview process to ensure that it was inclusive and equitable?

5. What were some of the baseline metrics that Math Movers Inc. established for diversity and inclusion in their hiring process?

6. How did Math Movers Inc. incorporate feedback from employees to ensure that they were creating an inclusive workplace?

7. What benefits did Math Movers Inc. experience as a result of implementing equity-based hiring practices?

8. How can other companies learn from the example of Math Movers Inc. and promote diversity and inclusion in their own hiring practices?

Practice 1.2

Title

Standardized Interview Questions and Process: A Case Study on Creating an Inclusive and Equitable Hiring Process

Introduction

In recent years, the importance of diversity and inclusivity in the workplace has become increasingly apparent. Organizations are now seeking ways to create a more inclusive and equitable hiring process to attract and retain a diverse pool of candidates. This case study explores the implementation of standardized interview questions and structured interview processes in a mid-sized technology company, referred to as TechCorp, and evaluates the impact of these changes on the organization's interview process and candidate diversity.

Background

TechCorp, a mid-sized technology company, identified the need to improve their hiring process to promote diversity and inclusivity. They recognized that interviewer bias and subjective evaluations were negatively impacting their candidate selection process. TechCorp decided to implement standardized interview questions, structured interview processes, interview training, and resources for candidates, and to track interview metrics.

Implementation

1. Standardized Interview Questions and Structured Processes: TechCorp developed a set of standardized interview questions relevant to the job requirements, aimed at assessing candidates' skills and qualifications objectively. A scoring rubric was created to evaluate candidates' responses consistently, reducing the impact of subjective assessments.

2. Interview Training and Resources: TechCorp provided interview training to their hiring managers and recruiters to minimize interviewer bias. Candidates were also offered sample questions and feedback on their performance, leveling the playing field for all applicants.

3. Feedback from Candidates: TechCorp began soliciting feedback from candidates after their interviews, including concerns or suggestions for improvement, to identify areas for improvement and ensure inclusivity and equity.

4. Evaluation of Interview Metrics: The organization started tracking the diversity of the candidate pool, interview scores, and hiring rates to measure the effectiveness of the changes made to the interview process.

Results

After implementing these strategies, TechCorp observed the following improvements:

1. Increased Diversity: The diversity of the candidate pool improved significantly, leading to a more diverse and inclusive workforce.

2. Reduced Interviewer Bias: Standardized interview questions and structured processes minimized interviewer bias, resulting in a more consistent evaluation of candidates.

3. Improved Candidate Experience: Candidates reported a positive interview experience, with increased transparency and fairness in the evaluation process.

4. Identifiable Areas for Improvement: By tracking interview metrics, TechCorp was able to identify areas for improvement and measure the effectiveness of the changes made to their interview process.

Conclusion

By implementing standardized interview questions, structured interview processes, and evaluating interview metrics, TechCorp successfully created a more inclusive and equitable hiring process. This case study demonstrates the potential benefits of such an approach, including increased diversity, reduced interviewer bias, improved candidate experience, and the ability to identify areas for improvement. Organizations looking to promote diversity and inclusivity in their hiring process can consider adopting similar strategies to achieve their goals.

1. What challenges did TechCorp face in its hiring process before

implementing standardized interview questions and structured processes?

2. How did TechCorp develop and implement standardized interview questions and a scoring rubric to reduce interviewer bias and improve candidate evaluation?

3. What resources and training were provided to interviewers and candidates to support a more inclusive and equitable interview process?

4. How did TechCorp solicit and utilize feedback from candidates to improve their interview process?

5. What interview metrics did TechCorp track to evaluate the effectiveness of the changes made to their interview process?

6. How did the implementation of standardized interview questions and structured processes impact the diversity of TechCorp's candidate pool and workforce?

7. In what ways did TechCorp's new hiring strategies lead to a more positive candidate experience?

8. How can other organizations learn from TechCorp's case study to improve their own hiring processes and promote diversity and inclusivity?

9. What additional strategies could TechCorp consider to further enhance the inclusivity and equity of their hiring process?

10. How does a more diverse and inclusive workforce benefit TechCorp's overall performance, innovation, and decision-making?

Practice 1.3

Group Activity
Inclusive Hiring Criteria Workshop

Objective
To review and revise current hiring criteria and processes to be more inclusive and attract a diverse pool of candidates.

Materials Needed
1. Job descriptions and hiring criteria for various positions within the organization.
2. Flipchart or whiteboard for brainstorming and note-taking.
3. Markers or pens for writing.

Instructions
1. Divide participants into small groups, with each group focusing on a specific job description or position within the organization.

2. Instruct each group to review the current job descriptions and hiring criteria for their assigned position. Encourage them to consider whether the requirements are inclusive and not unnecessarily restrictive.

3. Ask each group to brainstorm ways to revise the job descriptions and requirements to focus on essential skills and qualifications, rather than limiting or traditional requirements.

4. Have each group discuss the possibility of implementing competency-based hiring for their assigned position. Encourage them to think about how to evaluate candidates based on their ability to perform job-related tasks, rather than relying on specific educational or work experience requirements.

5. Ask groups to consider how lived experiences, such as volunteering, personal projects, or community involvement, could be incorporated as qualifications for their assigned position.

THE SEARCH: EQUITY BASED HIRING

6. Have each group discuss the potential benefits of using structured interviews that focus on specific competencies or skills required for the job, and how this could help minimize unconscious bias and provide a more objective evaluation of candidates.

7. Encourage groups to think about offering training and development opportunities for candidates who may not meet all qualifications but show potential and willingness to learn.

8. Finally, ask each group to identify diversity-focused metrics that could be used to track the diversity of the candidate pool and evaluate the effectiveness of their revised hiring criteria.

9. After the small group discussions, reconvene as a larger group and have each team present their findings and suggestions. Encourage a group discussion on the proposed changes and explore how they can be implemented across the organization.

10. After the workshop, assign a team to compile the suggestions and create an action plan for implementing the changes to the hiring criteria and processes within the organization.

Answer Key 1.1

1. Math Movers Inc. took several steps to promote diversity and inclusion in their hiring practices. They reviewed their job descriptions and made sure they were inclusive and not unnecessarily restrictive. They used a variety of channels to advertise job openings, including social media platforms and diversity-focused job boards. They attended diversity-focused career fairs and job events to connect with diverse candidates in person. They used competency-based hiring, evaluating candidates based on their ability to perform specific job-related tasks, and also considered lived experiences as a qualification for the job. They evaluated their interview process to ensure that it was inclusive and equitable, and regularly reviewed their hiring metrics to track the diversity of their applicant pool, interviewees, and new hires.

2. Math Movers Inc. adjusted their hiring criteria to be more inclusive of candidates from diverse backgrounds by focusing on the essential skills and qualifications needed for each job, rather than requirements that may limit the candidate pool. They used competency-based hiring, evaluating candidates based on their ability to perform specific job-related tasks, rather than relying on specific educational or work experience requirements. They also considered lived experiences, such as volunteering, personal projects, or community involvement, as a qualification for the job.

3. To attract a diverse pool of candidates for their job openings, Math Movers Inc. used a variety of channels to advertise job openings, including social media platforms such as LinkedIn, Twitter, and Facebook. They also partnered with organizations that serve underrepresented populations, such as minority professional associations, community-based organizations, and diversity-focused job boards. Math Movers Inc. attended diversity-focused career fairs and job events to connect with diverse candidates in person, and used them as an opportunity to network with potential candidates.

4. Math Movers Inc. evaluated their interview process to ensure that it was inclusive and equitable. They trained interviewers on unconscious biases and provided them with tools to recognize and avoid it. They used standardized interview questions and structured interview processes that involved a set of standardized questions and a scoring rubric to evaluate candidates' responses. They offered interview training and resources to candidates, such as sample questions and feedback on their performance, to level the playing field and provide all candidates with equal opportunities to succeed in the interview process.

5. The baseline metrics that Math Movers Inc. established for diversity and inclusion in their hiring process included tracking demographic data such as gender, race, ethnicity, and age across different stages of the hiring process, such as the applicant pool, interviewees, and new hires. They used data analytics to track and analyze hiring metrics and identify patterns and trends over time. They regularly reviewed hiring metrics to ensure that they were making progress towards equity-based hiring and set targets and goals for diversity and inclusion in the hiring process.

6. Math Movers Inc. incorporated feedback from employees to ensure that they were creating an inclusive workplace. They conducted surveys, focus groups, and other forms of employee feedback to ensure that the organization was creating an environment where all employees felt valued and supported.

THE SEARCH: EQUITY BASED HIRING

7. As a result of implementing equity-based hiring practices, Math Movers Inc. created a more diverse and inclusive workplace that better reflected the communities they served. They attracted and retained a diverse pool of candidates, which brought a variety of benefits to the organization, such as increased innovation and improved decision-making. They also fostered a culture of inclusivity, which led to higher employee engagement and retention.

8. Other companies can learn from the example of Math Movers Inc. by reviewing their own hiring practices and identifying areas where they can promote diversity and inclusion. They can adjust their hiring criteria to be more inclusive of candidates from diverse backgrounds, use a variety of channels to attract a diverse pool of candidates, evaluate their interview process to ensure that it is inclusive and equitable, and regularly review their hiring metrics to track progress towards equity-based hiring. Companies can also incorporate feedback from employees to ensure that they are creating an inclusive workplace and fostering

Answer Key 1.2

1. Before implementing standardized interview questions and structured processes, TechCorp faced challenges such as interviewer bias, subjective evaluations, and a lack of diversity in their candidate pool and workforce.

2. TechCorp developed a set of standardized interview questions that were relevant to the job requirements and focused on assessing candidates' skills and qualifications objectively. They also created a scoring rubric to consistently evaluate candidates' responses, which helped reduce the impact of subjective assessments.

3. TechCorp provided interview training to their hiring managers and recruiters to minimize interviewer bias. They also offered candidates sample questions and feedback on their performance, ensuring equal opportunities for all applicants to succeed in the interview process.

4. TechCorp solicited feedback from candidates after their interviews, including concerns or suggestions for improvement. This information helped the company identify areas for improvement and ensured their interview process remained inclusive and equitable.

5. TechCorp tracked interview metrics such as the diversity of the candidate pool, interview scores, and hiring rates to measure the effectiveness of the changes made to their interview process and to identify areas for improvement.

6. The implementation of standardized interview questions and structured processes led to a significant improvement in the diversity of TechCorp's candidate pool and workforce, resulting in a more diverse and inclusive environment.

7. TechCorp's new hiring strategies led to a more positive candidate experience by providing increased transparency and fairness in the evaluation process. Candidates felt better equipped to succeed in the interview process due to the resources and feedback provided.

8. Other organizations can learn from TechCorp's case study by adopting similar strategies such as implementing standardized interview questions, structured processes, providing resources and training for interviewers and candidates, soliciting feedback, and tracking interview metrics to promote diversity and inclusivity in their hiring processes.

Answer Key 1.2 (cont.)

9. Additional strategies TechCorp could consider to further enhance the inclusivity and equity of their hiring process include implementing blind recruitment techniques, expanding their talent sourcing strategies to reach underrepresented groups, and fostering a more inclusive company culture that values diversity and supports employee growth and development.

10. A more diverse and inclusive workforce benefits TechCorp's overall performance, innovation, and decision-making by bringing a variety of perspectives, experiences, and ideas to the table. This diversity can lead to increased creativity, better problem-solving, and more effective collaboration, ultimately contributing to the company's success.

THE SEARCH: EQUITY BASED HIRING

"The Invitation"

Dear Boss,

I remember when I got the invitation to interview, I was hyped, nervous, and curious all at the same time. I wanted to learn more about you, the organization, and its diverse employees so I checked out your homepage and was impressed by all your staff with chocolate skin and textured hair like mine. I wondered if it was smoke and mirrors.

When I walked in the room on interview day, I first noticed your team and was instantly struck. I saw faces that looked just like mine and felt motivated and ready. Your website was more than stock photos and I felt a sense of relief as I smiled inwardly. When I got the job offer, I was excited to start my new role and become part of your team.

But then, I got let down when I realized that there was no effort put into making my onboarding experience great. The folks I was connecting with on the committee weren't even from my department, and it took weeks for me to meet with you. Even then, you didn't really discuss expectations or priorities, and I couldn't help but wonder how important I was to the organization, how important I was to you. I felt like without early investment in my growth and development, how could you make sure I was successful?

I was on the lookout for symbols, words, and actions that would make me feel like I belonged, but they were nowhere to be found. The hype I felt on interview day faded as I struggled to find my place within our organization. In the end, my best day was my interview day, and my last day comes only one year later.

Sincerely,

Fatima

Chapter 2
Symbolic Interaction

The Symbolic Interaction framework is a theory created by a group of sociologists in the early 1900s. The main idea is that individuals create meaning through their interactions with others. They use symbols, like language, gestures, and objects, to communicate with each other and create shared understanding.

One of the main founders of the Symbolic Interactionist perspective was George Herbert Mead. He was interested in how individuals interact with each other and create meaning through their social interactions. Another important sociologist in this theory was Charles Cooley, who came up with the concept of the "looking-glass self." This means that our sense of self is shaped by how we believe others see us.

Herbert Blumer was a student of Mead's and helped to further develop the Symbolic Interactionist perspective. He focused on how social movements and collective behavior are shaped by the interactions of individuals.

Together, these sociologists created the Symbolic Interaction framework, which helps us understand how symbols and interactions shape our behavior and society. It's important to remember that the way we interact with others and the symbols we use can have a big impact on how we understand the world around us.

Symbolic Interaction is a crucial concept for leaders to understand because it has a significant impact on how people communicate and interact with one another in different environments, including the workplace. When hiring new employees, candidates use various symbols such as their appearance, tone of voice, and language to try to create a particular impression or meaning for the interviewer. These symbols can either enhance or diminish their chances of being selected for the job.

As an interviewer, it's also essential to be aware of the symbols being used, and to understand their meaning. This can include the candidate's body language, facial expressions, and the questions they ask. By being mindful of these symbolic interactionism, you can make more informed decisions about the candidates you are considering.

The Symbolic Interaction theory also helps to explain how individuals create their own sense of identity and self-concept through their interactions with others at work. This means that how we perceive ourselves is shaped by the feedback we receive from others and the symbols they use to convey their perceptions of us. For example, if we receive positive feedback from others, we are likely to have a more positive self-concept.

As a new or experienced leader, understanding Symbolic Interaction theory can help you create a more positive and inclusive workplace culture. By being mindful of the symbols that people use to communicate, you can build stronger relationships with your team, foster open communication, and ensure that everyone feels seen, valued and heard.

Can symbolic interactionism work against you?

Yes, symbolic interactionism can work against an individual if it leads to negative labeling and reinforces stereotypes. When people categorize or label others based on their perceived characteristics, it can have a significant impact on the way those individuals are treated and perceived by others. This can lead to a self-fulfilling prophecy, where the labeled individuals internalize the stereotypes and start to behave in ways that are consistent with the label.

For example, if an employee is labeled as "troublemaker" by their boss, the employee may internalize that label and start to behave in ways that reinforce it. The leader may then treat the employee differently, which can result in a negative cycle of behavior and treatment.

In this way, symbolic interactionism can work against individuals by reinforcing negative stereotypes and leading to negative outcomes. It is important to be aware of the impact of labeling and to take steps to reduce the negative effects of symbolic interactionism. This can be done by promoting positive labeling, increasing cultural awareness and understanding, and encouraging open and honest communication.

Symbolic interaction can also help explain the importance of onboarding and the role it plays in shaping an employee's relationship with their organization. The onboarding process is a time when new employees are introduced to the shared symbols, values, and beliefs that shape the organization's culture. By providing a positive and supportive onboarding experience, an organization can help new employees feel like they belong and are valued members of the team. I call this the First Nine Hours construct.

First Nine Hours

Thinking like a compass for the onboard experience of diverse new hires means taking a holistic approach to onboarding that considers all aspects of an employee's journey within the organization. By breaking the process down into my COMPASS Onboarding Experience framework, you can create a comprehensive onboarding experience that covers Connection, Onboarding, Motivation, Politics, Achievement, Setup, and Systems. This approach aligns well with the "First Nine Hours" concept and Simon Sinek's "why" notion.

The "First Nine Hours" concept emphasizes the significance of the initial phase when a new employee joins an organization, team, and work setting. This period allows the individual to connect with the company's brand, culture, and physical environment, establishing a solid basis for a fruitful and meaningful connection with the organization. During this stage, Simon Sinek's "why" notion is especially pertinent, as it assists the individual in grasping the organization's purpose and values, ultimately fostering their motivation and dedication.

Examining the employee's experience during the First Nine Hours through the lens of symbolic interaction provides insight into the power

The Invitation: Symbolic Interaction

dynamics at play, which can be addressed in the "Politics" component of the COMPASS Onboarding Experience framework. When a company invests in an employee's growth and development during this time, it sends a symbolic message that the employee is valued and significant. This message can shape the employee's perception of their relationship with the company and their motivation to contribute to its objectives. Conversely, a lack of investment in an employee's growth and development may lead to feelings of being undervalued and unmotivated.

Furthermore, the idea of symbolic interaction has broader implications for understanding the impact of symbols, communication, and interpretation on an individual's experience within their social environment, including their workplace. The symbols, words, and actions encountered in a person's work setting can influence their perception of their role and relationship with the organization. By incorporating these concepts into the COMPASS Onboarding Experience framework, you can create a more inclusive, supportive, and engaging onboarding experience that helps diverse new hires thrive.

In the case of Fatima's letter to her boss, the relevance of symbols becomes apparent. Fatima sought symbols, words, and actions that would help her feel a sense of belonging within the organization. By acknowledging and addressing these symbols, the organization could have enhanced Fatima's experience, boosting her motivation and commitment to the company. How might we consider the Compass Orientation Experience framework to ensure new employees are maximized starting on day one.

In this framework:

1. Connection emphasizes building relationships and networking within the company, promoting a sense of belonging and support.
2. Onboarding focuses on introducing new employees to the company's history, mission, culture, and values, ensuring they have a solid understanding of the organization.
3. Motivation encourages new hires to discover their "why," aligning their individual motivations with the company's purpose and values.

4. Politics addresses symbolic interaction and power dynamics in the workplace, helping employees navigate their roles and relationships effectively.

5. Achievement supports personal growth and development, offering resources for continuous learning, mentorship, and feedback.

6. Setup covers both the physical environment and the company's policies and procedures, ensuring new employees understand expectations and feel comfortable in their workspaces.

7. Systems provide new hires with the necessary tools, resources, and training to be successful in their roles, fostering productivity and efficiency from the start.

By adopting the COMPASS Onboarding Experience framework, you can create an inclusive, supportive, and engaging onboarding experience that helps diverse new hires thrive in your organization.

C - Connection

Building Relationships and Networking

- Icebreaker activities and team-building exercises
- Introduction to key team members and stakeholders
- Informal networking opportunities (e.g., lunches, coffee breaks)
- Collaboration and communication tools

Connection, as a significant component of building relationships and networking, plays a vital role in both personal and professional development. By engaging in icebreaker activities and team-building exercises, individuals can foster a sense of camaraderie and trust, which in turn leads to enhanced collaboration and productivity. Furthermore, introducing key team members and stakeholders facilitates the establishment of open lines of communication, enabling individuals to leverage one another's expertise and skills for mutual benefit. Additionally, informal networking opportunities such as lunches and coffee breaks provide a relaxed atmosphere for forging new connections and strengthening existing ones, promoting a sense of unity and collective purpose. Lastly, the incorporation of collaboration and communication tools empowers team members to work seamlessly and efficiently, fostering an environment that encourages innovation, problem-solving, and shared growth. In essence, the Connection component serves as the foundation for nurturing thriving professional relationships and networks, driving individual and organizational success.

O - Onboarding

Introduction and Orientation

- Welcome and introductions
- Company history and mission
- Organizational structure and hierarchy
- Overview of the company culture and values
- Explanation of the significance of the First Nine Hours

The Onboarding component, consisting of introduction and orientation, is a crucial aspect of integrating new employees into a company. A warm welcome and proper introductions set the stage for a positive working relationship, while providing insights into the company's history and mission offers context for the employee's role in the organization. By outlining the organizational structure and hierarchy, new hires gain a clear understanding of reporting lines and decision-making processes, which in turn enables them to navigate the workplace effectively. Furthermore, an overview of the company culture and values not only aligns employees with the organization's ethos but also fosters a sense of belonging and pride. The emphasis on the First Nine Hours signifies the importance of a strong start, allowing new employees to quickly acclimate and begin making meaningful contributions. Ultimately, a well-executed onboarding process enhances employee engagement, satisfaction, and retention, leading to a more productive and cohesive workforce that can drive organizational success.

M - Motivation

Discovering the "Why"

- Presentation on Simon Sinek's "why" concept
- Exploration of the company's purpose and values
- Personal reflection on individual motivations and alignment with the company's mission
- Group discussions on the company's "why" and its relevance to individual roles

The Motivation component, centered around discovering the "why," is essential in fostering a deep sense of purpose and commitment among employees. By introducing concepts like Simon Sinek's "why," individuals are encouraged to reflect on the underlying reasons that drive them and their connection to the company's mission. Exploring the organization's purpose and values not only reinforces a shared vision but also helps employees understand their role in achieving the company's objectives. Personal reflection on individual motivations and alignment with the company's mission allows employees to find meaning in their work, which in turn leads to increased job satisfaction and productivity. Engaging in group discussions about the company's "why" and its relevance to individual roles further emphasizes the significance of each employee's contribution to the organization's success. Ultimately, the Motivation component plays a pivotal role in creating a passionate and dedicated workforce, driven by a shared understanding of the company's purpose and empowered to make a meaningful impact.

P - Politics

Symbolic Interaction and Power Dynamics

- Introduction to symbolic interaction theory
- Discussion of symbols, communication, and interpretation in the workplace
- Identifying power dynamics at play
- Strategies for enhancing positive symbolic interactionism

The Politics component, focusing on symbolic interaction and power dynamics, is a significant aspect of navigating workplace relationships and ensuring effective communication. Introducing employees to the symbolic interaction theory provides a framework for understanding how meaning is constructed and interpreted within the organization, shaping the way individuals interact and relate to one another. Discussing symbols, communication, and interpretation in the workplace enhances employees' awareness of the subtle cues and messages that can impact relationships, collaboration, and decision-making. By identifying power dynamics at play, employees become better equipped to recognize potential barriers to effective communication, collaboration, and innovation. Developing strategies for enhancing positive symbolic interactionism fosters an inclusive and transparent environment, where all employees feel empowered to contribute their ideas and perspectives. The Politics component is crucial for cultivating a workplace culture that values open communication, respect, and collaboration, ultimately contributing to individual and organizational success.

A - Achievement

Personal Growth and Development (Part A)

- Overview of available training and development opportunities
- Personal goal-setting and development planning
- Mentorship and coaching programs
- Opportunities for feedback and performance reviews

Ongoing Support and Feedback (Part B)

- Regular check-ins with managers or mentors
- Opportunities for continuous learning and development
- Channels for providing feedback and suggestions
- Celebrating milestones and achievements

The Achievement component, encompassing personal growth and development as well as ongoing support and feedback, plays a vital role in fostering a thriving and engaged workforce. By providing an overview of available training and development opportunities, employees are empowered to take charge of their own growth and enhance their skills and expertise. Personal goal-setting and development planning enable individuals to align their aspirations with the organization's objectives, fostering a sense of purpose and commitment. Mentorship and coaching programs provide tailored guidance and support, equipping employees with the tools and resources to excel in their roles. Opportunities for feedback and performance reviews contribute to continuous improvement and self-awareness.

The second part of the Achievement component, ongoing support and feedback, is equally important. Regular check-ins with managers or mentors ensure that employees receive timely guidance and reinforcement, while continuous learning and development opportunities promote a culture of adaptability and innovation. Establishing channels for providing feedback and suggestions encourages open communication and empowers employees to contribute to the betterment of the organization. Celebrating milestones and achievements not only acknowledges hard work and dedication but also fosters a sense of pride and motivation among team members. Ultimately, the Achievement component is instrumental in nurturing a high-performing and growth-oriented workforce, driving both individual and organizational success.

S - Setup

Physical Environment and Workspace (Part A)

- Office tour and workstation setup
- Review of safety and security protocols
- Introduction to company facilities and amenities
- Overview of remote work policies and procedures (if applicable)

Company Policies and Procedures (Part B)

- Overview of HR policies (e.g., benefits, leave, harassment, diversity)
- Review of company-specific procedures and protocols
- Compliance and legal requirements
- Reporting and escalation processes

The Setup component, comprising the physical environment and workspace as well as company policies and procedures, is crucial for establishing a comfortable, safe, and efficient work environment. In Part A, an office tour and workstation setup enable employees to familiarize themselves with their surroundings, ensuring they have the necessary tools and resources to work effectively. Reviewing safety and security protocols instills a sense of security and confidence, while introducing company facilities and amenities demonstrates a commitment to employee well-being. An overview of remote work policies and procedures, if applicable, provides guidance and support for maintaining productivity and communication in a flexible work arrangement.

In Part B, the focus shifts to company policies and procedures, which are equally significant. Providing an overview of HR policies such as benefits, leave, harassment, and diversity ensures that employees understand their rights and responsibilities within the organization. Reviewing company-specific procedures and protocols helps employees navigate the unique aspects of their workplace, while compliance and legal requirements emphasize the importance of adhering to established rules and regulations. Clear reporting and escalation processes empower employees to address concerns and contribute to a transparent and accountable work culture. Ultimately, the Setup component lays the groundwork for a conducive and well-organized work environment, promoting employee satisfaction, productivity, and success.

S - Systems

Tools, Systems, and Resources

- Training on company software and technology
- Overview of internal communication channels
- Access to necessary resources and materials
- IT support and troubleshooting

The Systems component, which encompasses tools, systems, and resources, is a critical aspect of enabling employees to work efficiently and effectively within an organization. Providing training on company software and technology equips team members with the knowledge and skills required to navigate and utilize essential tools, thereby enhancing productivity and collaboration. An overview of internal communication channels fosters seamless communication and information-sharing among employees, ensuring that everyone stays informed and connected. Ensuring access to necessary resources and materials empowers employees to complete their tasks with confidence and competence, further contributing to individual and team success.

In addition, IT support and troubleshooting are invaluable for maintaining a smooth workflow and minimizing disruptions caused by technical issues. By offering timely assistance and solutions, employees can focus on their core responsibilities and maintain a high level of productivity. Ultimately, the Systems component plays a pivotal role in optimizing the work environment and facilitating the successful execution of tasks and projects, driving organizational growth and success.d engaging onboarding experience for new employees, organizations lay the groundwork for a resilient and flourishing workplace.

In summary, by crafting a supportive and engaging onboarding experience for new employees, organizations lay the groundwork for a resilient and flourishing workplace. This approach not only instills a sense of value and connection in new hires from the outset but also nurtures a strong sense of belonging, motivation, and dedication to the organization's mission and values. By investing wholeheartedly in a comprehensive and thoughtful onboarding process, companies can inspire a thriving work environment, bolster employee retention, and propel long-term success for both the individuals and the organization as a whole.

The Invitation: Symbolic Interaction

Key Questions

How would you explain Symbolic Interaction to a peer?

Symbolic Interaction is a sociological theory that emphasizes the role of symbols, language, and interaction in shaping people's understanding of the world around them.

How can understanding Symbolic Interaction theory impact the hiring process?

By being aware of the symbolic meanings behind interactions during the hiring process, individuals involved can make more informed decisions and create a more equitable and effective hiring process.

What are some symbols that candidates may use during a job interview?

Candidates may use symbols such as their clothing, tone of voice, and body language to convey a particular impression during a job interview.

How can personal biases affect the hiring process?

Personal biases can influence the interpretations of symbols during the hiring process, leading to inaccurate or unfair decisions.

What is the importance of Symbolic Interaction theory in the context of African Americans?

Symbolic Interaction theory highlights the importance of cultural and symbolic messages received by African Americans and how they navigate and respond to those messages in their interactions with others. It also highlights the importance of social status and power dynamics in shaping their experiences.

How can Symbolic Interaction theory be applied to hiring processes?

Symbolic Interaction theory can be applied to hiring processes by understanding how symbols are used by job applicants and interviewers to convey information about themselves and their perceptions of each other. By being aware of the symbolic meanings behind these interactions, hiring managers and decision-makers can make more informed and fair decisions. It also emphasizes the importance of managing personal biases and understanding the subjective interpretations of symbols in the hiring process.

In what ways do Black Americans face negative stereotypes and how do they respond to them according to Symbolic Interactionism?

Black Americans often face negative racial stereotypes in the media and in their interactions with others. These stereotypes can have a profound impact on how they are perceived and treated by others. Symbolic Interactionism highlights how Black Americans may challenge and resist these negative stereotypes by constructing new symbolic meanings that reinforce their positive self-image. It also emphasizes the importance of social status and power dynamics in shaping the experiences of Black Americans, as the ways in which they are treated and the opportunities available to them are often influenced by those in positions of authority.

How can the principles of Symbolic Interactionism be used to improve communication and relationships with others?

By being aware of the symbolic meanings behind our actions and words, we can improve our communication skills and build stronger, more meaningful relationships with others. Symbolic Interactionism emphasizes the importance of understanding how people create meaning through their interactions with others, and how this can shape our understanding of the world around us. By being mindful of the symbolic interactions we have with others, we can improve our communication and build better relationships.

Symbolic Interaction is a powerful tool for understanding how people communicate and interact with each other in a variety of settings. By being aware of the symbolic meanings behind our actions and words, we can improve our communication skills and build stronger, more meaningful relationships with others while understanding the complex ways in which diverse candidates navigate and respond to the symbolic and cultural messages they receive in their interactions with others.

Practice 2.1

A new employee named Maria starts at an organization, and she is the only Hispanic employee in her department. On her first day, her coworkers use Spanish words and make jokes about her culture. Although they meant the jokes to be friendly, Maria feels embarrassed and uncomfortable.

In this scenario, the coworkers are using symbols (Spanish words and cultural jokes) to interact with Maria, and these symbols have a significant impact on Maria's experiences and perceptions. The coworkers believe that their use of Spanish words and cultural jokes is a friendly gesture, but for Maria, these symbols are associated with negative stereotypes and discrimination. This is an example of how symbols can be interpreted differently based on an individual's experiences and perspectives, and how symbolic interaction can shape the experiences and perceptions of individuals in the workplace.

1. How did the symbols used by Maria's coworkers impact her experience and sense of belonging in the workplace?

2. How might Maria's experience be different if she was not the only Hispanic employee in her department?

3. How might the use of Spanish words and cultural jokes contribute to a larger pattern of discrimination or microaggressions in the workplace?

4. What steps can the organization take to educate employees on the impact of their language and behavior on their coworkers, and to promote a more inclusive and respectful workplace culture?

5. How can the principles of symbolic interaction be used to create a more positive and supportive workplace culture for all employees, regardless of their background or identity?

6. How can organizations ensure that their employees are aware of cultural differences and are respectful towards them?

7. How might the negative impact of the symbols used by Maria's coworkers affect her job performance, productivity, and overall well-being?

8. What role does communication play in shaping the use of symbols in the workplace? How can organizations encourage open and respectful communication between employees?

9. What are the legal implications of using symbols that may be interpreted as discriminatory or offensive in the workplace? How can organizations ensure that their policies and practices are in line with legal requirements related to workplace discrimination?

10. How can organizations measure the effectiveness of their efforts to create a more inclusive and respectful workplace culture, and what steps can they take to continuously improve their approach?

Practice 2.2

Group Activity
Exploring Symbolic Interaction in the Workplace

Objective
To understand the impact of Symbolic Interaction on communication and interpersonal relationships in the workplace, and to develop strategies for creating a more positive and inclusive work environment.

Materials Needed
1. Flipchart or whiteboard for brainstorming and note-taking.
2. Markers or pens for writing.
3. Handout with a brief overview of the Symbolic Interaction framework (optional).

Instructions
1. Begin by providing a brief introduction to the Symbolic Interaction framework and its relevance in the workplace. Distribute the handout if you have one prepared.

2. Divide participants into small groups of 3-4 people.

3. Ask each group to discuss and list examples of symbols and interactions they have encountered in the workplace. This can include verbal communication, body language, facial expressions, or other non-verbal cues.

4. Instruct each group to consider the impact of these symbols and interactions on their own behavior, self-concept, and workplace relationships.

5. Next, ask each group to brainstorm strategies for being more mindful of the symbols they use in their interactions with colleagues and for interpreting the symbols used by others. Encourage them to think about how they can create a more inclusive and positive work environment through their communication and interactions.

The Invitation: Symbolic Interaction

6. After the small group discussions, reconvene as a larger group and have each team present their findings and strategies. Facilitate a group discussion on the impact of Symbolic Interaction in the workplace and how understanding this concept can benefit leaders and employees alike.

7. Encourage participants to reflect on the following questions:

    - How can you apply the concept of Symbolic Interaction in your everyday interactions with colleagues?
    - What steps can you take to ensure that your communication is inclusive and mindful of the symbols being used?
    - How can you provide constructive feedback to others in a way that supports a positive self-concept and fosters growth?

8. Conclude the activity by summarizing the key takeaways and encouraging participants to implement the strategies discussed in their workplace interactions.

Practice 2.3

Group Activity
First Nine Hours Scavenger Hunt

Objective
To engage new employees in a fun, interactive way that helps them explore and internalize key aspects of the First Nine Hours framework.

Instructions

1. Divide new employees into small teams of 3-5 people. Provide each team with a scavenger hunt list that includes tasks and questions related to the First Nine Hours framework.

2. Allocate a specific time frame (e.g., 2 hours) for teams to complete the scavenger hunt.

3. The scavenger hunt list should include tasks and questions that cover all aspects of the First Nine Hours framework, such as:

   - Find and take a picture with the company's mission statement displayed in the office.
   - Identify and discuss one example of a company value in action.
   - Interview a team member about their role and how it aligns with the company's "why."
   - Locate an example of positive symbolic interaction in the workplace and explain its significance.
   - Set a personal goal for your first three months with the company and share it with your team.
   - Connect with a key stakeholder or team member and learn about their role within the organization.
   - Identify a safety or security protocol that is important for your role.
   - Find a resource or tool that you will use in your daily work and explain its purpose.
   - Review a company policy that is particularly relevant to your role and discuss its implications.
   - Share one piece of feedback or a suggestion for the company based on your initial impressions.

The Invitation: Symbolic Interaction

4. At the end of the allocated time, have each team present their findings and experiences to the larger group.

5. Facilitate a group discussion to debrief the scavenger hunt, highlighting key insights, and addressing any questions or concerns that emerged during the activity.

6. Conclude the activity by reinforcing the importance of the First Nine Hours framework and how it can contribute to a successful and fulfilling experience with the company.

By participating in this scavenger hunt, new employees will have the opportunity to actively explore and engage with the various aspects of the First Nine Hours framework, fostering a deeper understanding of the company culture, values, and resources available to them. This activity can contribute to a strong sense of belonging, motivation, and commitment to the organization.

Answer Key 2.1

1. The symbols used by Maria's coworkers likely made her feel uncomfortable, embarrassed, and like an outsider in the workplace. They may have also reinforced negative stereotypes and discrimination associated with her culture.

2. If Maria was not the only Hispanic employee in her department, she may have felt more supported and less singled out by her coworkers' use of Spanish words and cultural jokes. She may have also had other colleagues who shared her cultural background and could relate to her experiences.

3. The use of Spanish words and cultural jokes can contribute to a larger pattern of discrimination and microaggressions in the workplace, particularly if they are used in a way that reinforces negative stereotypes or belittles an individual's cultural identity.

4. The organization can provide training and education to employees on the impact of their language and behavior on their coworkers. They can also establish clear policies and guidelines for appropriate workplace conduct and provide resources for employees who experience discrimination or microaggressions.

5. The principles of symbolic interaction can be used to create a more positive and supportive workplace culture by promoting open and respectful communication, acknowledging and valuing diversity, and creating opportunities for all employees to contribute and succeed.

6. Organizations can ensure that their employees are aware of cultural differences and are respectful towards them by providing cultural awareness training, establishing clear policies and guidelines for appropriate workplace conduct, and promoting a culture of inclusivity and respect.

7. The negative impact of the symbols used by Maria's coworkers could affect her job performance, productivity, and overall well-being by creating a stressful and uncomfortable work environment.

8. Communication plays a critical role in shaping the use of symbols in the workplace. Organizations can encourage open and respectful communication between employees by establishing clear channels for feedback and dialogue and promoting a culture of transparency and collaboration.

9. There are legal implications associated with using symbols that may be interpreted as discriminatory or offensive in the workplace. Organizations must ensure that their policies and practices are in line with legal requirements related to workplace discrimination and harassment.

10. Organizations can measure the effectiveness of their efforts to create a more inclusive and respectful workplace culture through metrics such as employee satisfaction surveys, retention rates, and diversity metrics. They can continuously improve their approach by soliciting feedback from employees, monitoring trends in the industry, and adapting their strategies as needed.

"LABELS"

Dear Boss,

I wanted to bring to your attention an issue that has been bothering me since my first day on the job.

During my introduction to the team, you mentioned that I was a single mom and also mentioned that I am good at my job. While I appreciate the recognition of my abilities, I felt uncomfortable being labeled as a "single mom" in front of my colleagues. As a Black woman I felt the intersecting weights of your comment. The label was not relevant to my job performance, and it was not something I wanted to be known for in the workplace.

Unfortunately, my concerns were validated over the next few weeks as some of my colleagues made insensitive comments about single mothers. I felt isolated and frustrated because I was being judged based on my personal circumstances rather than my professional abilities. It affected my motivation and work performance, and I believe it could have been avoided if there was more understanding from my colleagues.

I believe that it's essential for colleagues to recognize each other's professional abilities and treat each other with respect and dignity, regardless of personal circumstances. As an alternative to improve the situation, it would have been great to have a group of individuals with similar circumstances to mine, so that we could connect and inspire each other.

Unfortunately, due to the conditions that were set, I feel that I cannot be successful in this work environment, and I have decided to resign.

Thank you for your understanding.

Sincerely,
Monique

Chapter 3
Affinity Grouping

Affinity groups are communities of individuals who share a common identity or interest and come together to provide mutual support, share knowledge and experiences, and advocate for their community. These groups are often based on specific characteristics, such as race, ethnicity, gender, sexuality, religion, disability, or profession.

Like the framework for equity-based hiring, the concept of affinity groups has its roots in the social movements of the 1960s and 1970s, particularly in the United States. During this time, various social movements, such as the civil rights movement, feminist movement, and anti-war movement, emerged and gained momentum.

As these movements grew, activists began to form small groups based on shared identities or interests. These groups, which were often referred to as "consciousness-raising" groups or "sisterhoods," provided a space for individuals to share their experiences and discuss the issues affecting their communities.

Over time, these groups evolved into what are now known as affinity groups. Affinity groups continue to be used in a variety of social movements, including environmental activism, LGBTQ+ rights, and anti-racism efforts, to name a few.

Affinity groups are for more than social movements, however, and can be used in various settings. These groups offer a brave space for members to share their stories, discuss common issues, and receive support and validation from others who understand their perspective. Members can collaborate to raise awareness about issues affecting their community, promote social justice and equity, and advocate for policy changes that support their rights and well-being.

Risk and Resilience

The Risk and Resilience Framework is a theoretical model that stems from a broad body of research on resilience and human development. It is used to comprehend how individuals deal with difficult circumstances and cope with adversity. The model is centered around two primary factors that influence an individual's ability to overcome challenges: risk factors and protective factors.

Risk factors are conditions or events that increase the likelihood of negative outcomes, such as poverty, trauma, or a lack of social support. Protective factors are conditions or events that promote positive outcomes, such as access to education, supportive relationships, and good mental and physical health.

The Risk and Resilience Framework suggests that individuals who are exposed to high levels of risk are more likely to experience negative outcomes, such as poor mental health, substance abuse, and criminal behavior. However, those who have strong protective factors are more likely to overcome these challenges and experience positive outcomes.

The framework highlights the importance of identifying and strengthening protective factors in individuals and communities, rather than just focusing on reducing risk factors. This approach acknowledges that people can overcome adversity and build resilience when they have access to supportive resources and relationships.

The Risk and Resilience Framework provides a valuable lens for understanding the challenges and opportunities faced by members of affinity groups at work. By recognizing the significance of both risk and protective factors and promoting resilience, affinity groups can help create a supportive and inclusive workplace culture where all employees can flourish.

Risk Factors

Affinity groups may face unique challenges related to discrimination, bias, and exclusion in the workplace. Understanding these risk factors can help affinity groups develop strategies to overcome them, such as advocating for policies that promote diversity and inclusion, and building networks of support within the organization.

An example of identifying risk factors for an affinity group in the workplace could be a group of Black women who may face discrimination, bias, and exclusion in their workplace. Some risk factors they may face include being overlooked for promotions or pay raises, having their ideas dismissed or attributed to others, and facing microaggressions or overt racism from colleagues.

By understanding these risk factors, the affinity group can develop strategies to overcome them, such as advocating for policies that promote diversity and inclusion, such as anti-bias training for all employees, creating a mentorship program for women of color, and ensuring that diversity and inclusion are key performance indicators for all managers.

The group can also work to build networks of support within the organization, such as creating a regular forum for women of color to share their experiences and support each other, and collaborating with other affinity groups and employee resource groups to create a more inclusive workplace culture. By doing so, the affinity group can mitigate the risks they face and create a more supportive and inclusive workplace for all employees.

To summarize, employees of color face various risk factors in the workplace that can affect their well-being and success, including discrimination, lack of representation, limited career advancement opportunities, wage disparities, and unsupportive work environments. These risk factors can impact the success and well-being of employees of color and create barriers to equity and inclusion in the workplace. Employers and organizations need to address these risk factors and create more supportive and inclusive work environments.

Protective Factors

Promoting protective factors and addressing risk factors can create more equitable and inclusive workplaces that benefit all employees, including those of color. Employers, organizations, and supervisors must take action to address these risk factors and promote protective factors to promote the success and well-being of employees of color.

Supervisors can play a crucial role in creating a supportive and inclusive workplace culture for their staff of color. To address risk and protective factors, supervisors can adopt various strategies. One such strategy is to address bias. Supervisors can educate themselves on the ways that bias can manifest in the workplace and create a culture that promotes equity and inclusion. This can include providing unconscious bias training, diverse hiring practices, and inclusive policies and practices.

Another strategy is to provide mentorship and sponsorship. Supervisors can identify career goals for their staff of color and provide opportunities for professional development. This can help employees of color overcome barriers to career advancement and build relationships with senior leaders. Encouraging employee resource groups such as affinity groups or diversity and inclusion committees is another strategy. These groups can provide a brave space for employees of color to connect with each other, share their experiences, and advocate for their needs and rights.

Promoting transparency and fairness is another strategy that supervisors can use to address risk and protective factors. Supervisors can provide clear performance expectations, regular feedback, and ensure that compensation practices are transparent and equitable. Supervisors can foster open communication by providing a brave space for employees of color to share their experiences and concerns. This can help supervisors understand the unique challenges that their staff of color may face and create strategies to address them.

Protective and promotive factors are both important in promoting resilience and positive outcomes in individuals, but they differ in their focus and approach. Protective factors are factors that mitigate the effects of risk factors or adverse life events, and promote positive outcomes. They are characteristics or resources that help individuals cope with challenges and setbacks, and maintain their well-being and success. Protective factors can include things like social support, positive relationships, coping skills, and access to resources and services.

Promotive Factors

Promotive factors, on the other hand, are factors that promote positive outcomes and well-being in the absence of adversity or risk. They are characteristics or resources that help individuals thrive and achieve their potential. Promotive factors can include things like self-esteem, positive identity, optimism, sense of purpose, and social and emotional competence.

While both protective and promotive factors are important in promoting resilience and positive outcomes, they differ in their focus and approach. Protective factors focus on mitigating the effects of risk and adversity, while promotive factors focus on promoting positive outcomes and well-being. Protective factors are more reactive, while promotive factors are more proactive.

Both protective and promotive factors can be useful in promoting resilience and positive outcomes in individuals, and can be incorporated into interventions and programs to promote well-being and success. By focusing on both protective and promotive factors, individuals can develop the skills and resources they need to thrive in the face of adversity and achieve their potential.

Affinity Groups in Action

Affinity groups can also work to build protective factors that promote resilience, such as cultivating supportive relationships within the group, developing skills and competencies that are valued in the workplace, and advocating for resources and support from the organization.

Let's explore an example of building protective factors for an affinity group in the workplace could be a group of LGBTQ+ employees who may face discrimination, bias, and exclusion in their workplace.

CULTIVATING SUPPORTIVE RELATIONSHIPS WITHIN THE GROUP

The LGBTQ+ affinity group can create a welcoming and supportive space where members can share their experiences, connect with each other, and offer mutual support. This can help members feel less isolated and more empowered to navigate the challenges they face.

DEVELOPING SKILLS AND COMPETENCIES THAT ARE VALUED IN THE WORKPLACE

The LGBTQ+ affinity group can organize workshops and training sessions that help members build skills and competencies that are highly valued in their workplace. For example, members can develop their leadership skills, public speaking skills, or project management skills, which can help them advance in their careers.

ADVOCATING FOR RESOURCES AND SUPPORT FROM THE ORGANIZATION

The LGBTQ+ affinity group can work to advocate for policies and practices that support their well-being and success in the workplace. This could include advocating for gender-neutral bathrooms, advocating for inclusive language in company policies, and advocating for comprehensive healthcare benefits that cover LGBTQ+ healthcare needs.

By building these protective factors, the LGBTQ+ affinity group can promote resilience, mitigate the risks they face, and create a more inclusive and supportive workplace culture.

The risk and resilience model emphasizes the importance of resilience in overcoming adversity. Affinity groups can work to build resilience by developing a sense of shared identity and purpose, promoting self-care and well-being, and advocating for policies and practices that support their goals and values.

Let's explore a second example of fostering resilience for an affinity group in the workplace could be a group of employees with disabilities who may face unique challenges related to accessibility, accommodation, and stigma. To foster resilience, the disability affinity group can:

DEVELOP A SENSE OF SHARED IDENTITY AND PURPOSE

The disability affinity group can develop a clear mission and vision that promotes the well-being and success of employees with disabilities. This can help members feel a sense of belonging and purpose, and work together towards common goals.

PROMOTE SELF-CARE AND WELL-BEING

The disability affinity group can promote self-care and well-being by organizing wellness activities, such as mindfulness sessions, yoga classes, or stress management workshops. These activities can help members manage the stress and challenges of the workplace, and promote mental and physical health.

ADVOCATE FOR POLICIES AND PRACTICES THAT SUPPORT THEIR GOALS AND VALUES:

The disability affinity group can advocate for policies and practices that promote inclusion and accessibility, such as accessible workspaces, flexible work arrangements, and reasonable accommodations for employees with disabilities. By advocating for these policies and practices, the group can promote the well-being and success of all employees with disabilities, and create a more inclusive and supportive workplace culture.

By fostering resilience in these ways, the disability affinity group can overcome adversity, promote well-being and success for employees with disabilities, and create a more inclusive and equitable workplace culture for all employees.

By applying the risk and resilience model to the challenges faced by affinity groups at work, organizations can support the well-being and success of their employees, promote diversity and inclusion, and create a more equitable and just workplace culture.

Affinity groups are important because they provide a safe and supportive space for individuals who share a common identity or interest to connect with each other, share their experiences and challenges, and advocate for their needs and rights. These groups can be especially important in workplaces and other settings where members may face discrimination, bias, or exclusion.

By promoting these protective factors, employers and organizations can create more equitable and inclusive workplaces that promote the success and well-being of all employees, including employees of color.

COMMUNITY OF CARE

Establishing a community of care entails cultivating a nurturing, inclusive, and supportive atmosphere in which individuals can flourish, feel appreciated, and form meaningful connections with others. This type of community is founded on principles of empathy, mutual respect, and a sincere concern for the well-being of all members. Within the realms of professional and affinity group settings, fostering a community of care can yield numerous advantages.

In practice, a supportive environment might involve implementing mental health programs, offering flexible work arrangements, or encouraging work-life balance. Managers and coworkers can actively listen to one another, validate each other's emotions, and create safe spaces for sharing experiences. Encouraging self-care, offering stress-reduction activities, and connecting individuals to relevant resources can help alleviate stress, anxiety, and burnout.

To foster a sense of care and support, organizations can establish recognition programs that celebrate employees' achievements and contributions. Providing regular feedback, offering opportunities for growth, and involving employees in decision-making can boost motivation and commitment. It's essential to create a culture where employees feel valued, and their opinions are respected.

Open communication channels, regular team-building activities, and conflict resolution strategies can help build trust and respect among team members. By promoting a culture of transparency and active listening, organizations can create an environment where individuals feel comfortable expressing their ideas and concerns, leading to more effective problem-solving and collaboration.

Higher retention and loyalty: To increase retention and loyalty, organizations can prioritize employee satisfaction by offering competitive compensation packages, opportunities for career advancement, and benefits tailored to employees' needs. Consistently demonstrating care and appreciation for employees can help foster a sense of loyalty to the organization.

Opportunities for personal and professional growth can be provided through mentorship programs, skills development workshops, and opportunities for employees to take on new challenges or responsibilities. Encouraging knowledge-sharing and creating a culture of continuous learning can help individuals learn from one another and grow both personally and professionally.

Cultivating a community of care involves creating a nurturing, inclusive, and supportive atmosphere that allows individuals to flourish, feel valued, and form meaningful connections. This community is built on empathy, mutual respect, and genuine concern for everyone's well-being. In professional and affinity group settings, a community of care can offer numerous benefits such as improved mental health, increased engagement, enhanced collaboration, higher retention, and personal and professional growth. By implementing supportive measures, fostering open communication, providing growth opportunities, and promoting social connections, organizations can create an environment where individuals feel connected, valued, and motivated, ultimately contributing to their overall well-being and satisfaction.

Labels: Affinity Grouping

Key Questions

What are affinity groups?

Affinity groups are communities of individuals who share a common identity or interest and come together to provide mutual support, share knowledge and experiences, and advocate for their community.

What is the Risk and Resilience Framework?

The Risk and Resilience Framework is a theoretical model that suggests individuals who are exposed to high levels of risk are more likely to experience negative outcomes, but those who have strong protective factors are more likely to overcome challenges and experience positive outcomes.

How can affinity groups identify risk factors in the workplace?

Affinity groups can identify risk factors by understanding the unique challenges they may face related to discrimination, bias, and exclusion in the workplace. This can help them develop strategies to overcome these risks, such as advocating for policies that promote diversity and inclusion and building networks of support within the organization.

What are some protective factors that can promote the success and well-being of employees of color?

Protective factors include inclusive workplace culture, mentorship and sponsorship, affinity groups and networks, transparent and fair compensation practices, and access to resources and benefits.

What role do supervisors play in creating a supportive and inclusive workplace culture for employees of color?

Supervisors play a critical role in addressing risk and protective factors for employees of color by promoting equity and inclusion, providing mentorship and sponsorship, encouraging employee resource groups, promoting transparency and fairness, and fostering open communication.

Why is it important to address risk factors and promote protective factors for employees of color in the workplace?

Addressing risk factors and promoting protective factors can create more equitable and inclusive workplaces that benefit all employees, including those of color, and promote their success and well-being.

Practice 3.1

A company called Diversity Co. recognized the unique challenges faced by employees of color in the workplace. They decided to establish an affinity group specifically for employees of color, with the goal of providing a safe and supportive space where members could connect, share their experiences, and advocate for their needs and rights.

The affinity group for employees of color was initially met with some resistance from senior leadership, who were concerned that it could be divisive or exclusionary. However, the group's organizers made it clear that the group was intended to complement, rather than replace, the company's broader diversity and inclusion initiatives. They emphasized that the group was open to all employees of color, regardless of their job function or seniority level.

As the affinity group began to establish itself, members felt more connected and supported in the workplace. They held regular meetings where they could discuss their experiences and share strategies for navigating the workplace. They also organized events to celebrate and promote the diverse cultures and perspectives of members, such as potlucks, cultural performances, and guest speakers.

Over time, the affinity group for employees of color proved to be a valuable asset to the company. Members felt more empowered to speak up about issues that affected them, and the group's advocacy efforts helped to drive positive change in the workplace. The group also helped to build stronger connections and understanding among employees of different racial backgrounds, contributing to a more inclusive and equitable workplace culture.

Thanks to the success of the affinity group for employees of color, Diversity Co. went on to establish similar groups for other affinity communities, such as LGBTQ+ employees and employees with disabilities. The company became known as a leader in promoting diversity and inclusion in the workplace, thanks in large part to the efforts of its affinity groups.

LABELS: AFFINITY GROUPING

1. What was the goal of the affinity group for employees of color at Diversity Co.?
2. How did senior leadership initially respond to the idea of the affinity group?
3. What did the organizers of the affinity group emphasize to senior leadership?
4. How did the affinity group for employees of color help members feel more connected and supported in the workplace?
5. What types of events did the affinity group organize to celebrate and promote diverse cultures and perspectives?
6. How did the affinity group's advocacy efforts help to drive positive change in the workplace?
7. What impact did the affinity group for employees of color have on building stronger connections and understanding among employees of different racial backgrounds?
8. How did the success of the affinity group for employees of color lead to the establishment of similar groups for other affinity communities?
9. How did Diversity Co. become known as a leader in promoting diversity and inclusion in the workplace?
10. What lessons can other companies learn from the success of Diversity Co.'s affinity groups?

Practice 3.2

Group Activity
Building Protective and Promotive Factors in the Workplace

Objective
To understand and implement strategies for promoting protective and promotive factors in the workplace, creating a more inclusive environment for employees of color and other underrepresented groups.

Materials Needed
1. Flipchart or whiteboard for brainstorming and note-taking.
2. Markers or pens for writing.
3. Handout with a brief overview of the Symbolic Interaction framework (optional).

Instructions
1. Begin by providing a brief introduction to protective and promotive factors and their relevance in the workplace. Distribute the handout if you have one prepared.
2. Divide participants into small groups of 4-5 people.
3. Instruct each group to discuss the importance of addressing bias in the workplace and brainstorm strategies for promoting equity and inclusion, such as unconscious bias training, diverse hiring practices, and inclusive policies.
4. Ask each group to consider the role of mentorship and sponsorship in supporting employees of color and other underrepresented groups. Encourage them to discuss strategies for providing professional development opportunities and fostering relationships with senior leaders.
5. Have each group discuss the benefits of employee resource groups, such as affinity groups or diversity and inclusion committees, and how they can provide support and advocacy for employees of color.

Labels: Affinity Grouping

6. Instruct groups to explore strategies for promoting transparency and fairness in the workplace, including clear performance expectations, regular feedback, and equitable compensation practices.

7. After the small group discussions, reconvene as a larger group and have each team present their findings and strategies. Facilitate a group discussion on the importance of building protective and promotive factors in the workplace and how these strategies can contribute to a more inclusive and supportive environment.

8. Encourage participants to reflect on the following questions:

    - How can you incorporate protective and promotive factors into your workplace culture and practices?
    - What steps can you take to ensure that employees of color and other underrepresented groups feel seen, valued, and supported in your organization?
    - How can you create opportunities for professional development and growth for employees from diverse backgrounds?

9. Conclude the activity by summarizing the key takeaways and encouraging participants to implement the strategies discussed in their workplace to create a more inclusive and supportive environment for all employees.

Practice 3.3

Group Activity
Building Empathy and Active Listening Skills

Objective
This exercise aims to help participants develop empathy and active listening skills, which are crucial for establishing a community of care.

Materials Needed
Paper and pen for each participant, a timer

Duration
30-45 minutes

Instructions

1. Divide participants into pairs.
2. Provide each participant with a piece of paper and a pen.
3. Explain the concept of empathy and active listening, emphasizing the importance of understanding others' perspectives, feelings, and needs, and genuinely engaging in the conversation.
4. Instruct each pair to decide who will be Partner A and Partner B.
5. Set a timer for 5 minutes. During this time, Partner A will share a personal or work-related experience with Partner B. Partner B's role is to actively listen without interrupting, asking questions, or offering advice.
6. After 5 minutes, ask Partner B to take 2 minutes to reflect on what they heard, summarize the key points, and share their understanding of Partner A's feelings and perspective.
7. Give Partner A 1 minute to provide feedback on Partner B's summary and understanding, clarifying any misunderstandings or highlighting any missed points.

Labels: Affinity Grouping

8. Switch roles, with Partner B sharing an experience, and repeat steps 5-7.

9. After both partners have shared their experiences and practiced active listening, bring the whole group together for a debrief.

10. Facilitate a group discussion, asking participants to share their insights and learning from the exercise. Discuss the challenges and benefits of active listening and empathizing, and how these skills can contribute to building a community of care.

This exercise can help participants understand the importance of empathy and active listening in fostering a supportive and caring environment, and provide them with practical experience in applying these skills.

Intersectional Leadership: Building Resilient Workforces

Answer Key 3.1

1. The goal of the affinity group for employees of color at Diversity Co. was to provide a safe and supportive space for members to connect, share their experiences, and advocate for their needs and rights.
2. Senior leadership initially responded to the idea of the affinity group with some resistance, as they were concerned that it could be divisive or exclusionary.
3. The organizers of the affinity group emphasized to senior leadership that the group was intended to complement, rather than replace, the company's broader diversity and inclusion initiatives. They also emphasized that the group was open to all employees of color, regardless of their job function or seniority level.
4. The affinity group for employees of color helped members feel more connected and supported in the workplace by holding regular meetings where they could discuss their experiences and share strategies for navigating the workplace.
5. The affinity group organized events such as potlucks, cultural performances, and guest speakers to celebrate and promote diverse cultures and perspectives.
6. The affinity group's advocacy efforts helped to drive positive change in the workplace by empowering members to speak up about issues that affected them.
7. The affinity group for employees of color had an impact on building stronger connections and understanding among employees of different racial backgrounds by promoting diversity, inclusion, and understanding in the workplace.
8. The success of the affinity group for employees of color led to the establishment of similar groups for other affinity communities, such as LGBTQ+ employees and employees with disabilities.
9. Diversity Co. became known as a leader in promoting diversity and inclusion in the workplace due to the efforts of its affinity groups.
10. Other companies can learn from the success of Diversity Co.'s affinity groups by recognizing the unique challenges faced by different affinity communities in the workplace, creating safe and supportive spaces for these communities to connect and advocate for their needs, and promoting diversity, equity, and inclusion throughout the organization.

Labels: Affinity Grouping

"Leveling"

Dear Boss,

I would like to express my concern and disappointment regarding an experience I had during my first day of training, specifically during the "cultural competency" session. While I have attended courses on related topics in the past, this was the first time I experienced a training in the workplace with an intentional focus on people of color with so few people of color. Still, I was excited for the conversation.

As I sat around the table with a group of teachers, I observed that some of them seemed exasperated at the goal of hiring and recruiting diverse talent. Upon being asked about my own hiring process, I enthusiastically shared my experience at the recruitment fair held at the Tacoma Dome, which eventually led to my letter of intent from this district and as a second career, but first year teacher, you can imagine my hopes and wishes for my very first classroom.

Unfortunately, my excitement was met with an unsettling comment from a new colleague, who bluntly mentioned that the district had planned to hire a "person of color" several months before the recruitment fair. This revelation left me feeling like a mere statistic, a token hire, rather than a valued and qualified professional. The reactions of some colleagues around the table, ranging from embarrassment to subtle dismissal of me and my ability, only served to exacerbate my discomfort.

I wanted to bring this matter to your attention because it is essential for me to convey that I am more than a number. I am a capable and qualified individual who has earned my place in this district through hard work, dedication, and passion for education. My diverse background and experiences have the potential to enrich my contributions to this school and to the students we serve.

I also was troubled during the whole group conversation on identity. One teacher asked the entire group what they call Black students, expressing confusion over the changing labels. She shared her experience of being corrected by students when using the terms "Black" and "African American." Unfortunately, her proposed solution was to refer to these students as "the dark ones." This comment is not only insensitive but also indicative of the need for further education and understanding in terms of cultural competence.

It is my hope that, moving forward, we can work together to foster an environment that values and respects the unique qualities and experiences of all staff members, regardless of their race or background.

Thank you for taking the time to read my concerns. I appreciate your understanding and any actions you may take to address this issue. I look forward to growing and learning in this district, and I am committed to giving my best to the students and the community we serve.

Sincerely,
Kim

Chapter 4
Equity & Justice

Recalling our definition of equity. Equity is a concept that emphasizes the importance of fairness and justice in the distribution of resources and opportunities. It recognizes that different individuals and groups may have different needs and experiences, and that these differences must be taken into account in order to create a more just and equitable society.

Equity can be seen as a byway to justice because it is a necessary precondition for achieving justice. Without equity, individuals and communities that are marginalized or disadvantaged may continue to face systemic barriers and discrimination that prevent them from accessing the resources and opportunities they need to thrive. By prioritizing equity, society can work towards a more just and inclusive future where all individuals have the opportunity to achieve their full potential.

To achieve equity, it is important to recognize and address the systemic barriers and discrimination that exist in society. This requires a commitment to challenging and dismantling systems of oppression and privilege, and working towards creating a more just and equitable society. It also requires listening to and centering the voices and experiences of individuals and communities that have been historically marginalized or disadvantaged.

In the workplace, equity can be promoted by implementing policies and practices that promote inclusive workplace cultures.Equity is a critical component of achieving justice in society. By prioritizing equity, society can work towards creating a more just and inclusive future where all individuals have the opportunity to thrive.

Anti-Oppression Framework

The Intersectional Anti-Oppression Framework is an approach that recognizes the interconnected nature of social identities and systems of oppression, and seeks to address the ways in which these intersecting identities create unique experiences of oppression and marginalization. This framework was developed by feminist scholar and activist Kimberlé Crenshaw, who coined the term "intersectionality" to describe the ways in which different social identities intersect and interact with systems of power and oppression.

The Intersectional Anti-Oppression Framework recognizes that individuals hold multiple social identities, such as race, gender, sexuality, class, ability, and religion, and that these identities can interact in complex and intersecting ways to shape their experiences of oppression and privilege. This framework seeks to address these intersecting systems of oppression and promote equity and social justice for all individuals, regardless of their social identities.

The Intersectional Anti-Oppression Framework has several key principles:

1. Recognizing the interconnected nature of social identities and systems of oppression.
2. Addressing the unique experiences of oppression and marginalization that result from the intersection of different social identities.
3. Promoting equity and social justice by addressing systems of power and privilege.
4. Centering the voices and experiences of marginalized individuals and communities.
5. Recognizing and challenging the ways in which dominant narratives and structures reinforce systems of oppression.

This framework can be applied in a variety of settings to promote equity and social justice for all individuals and can be a useful tool for employers who are committed to building a resilient workforce.

Addressing Systemic Barriers

Employers can use the anti-oppression framework to identify and address systemic barriers that prevent individuals from diverse backgrounds from entering and succeeding in the workforce. This can include barriers related to hiring practices, promotion, and retention.

Conducting a Diversity Audit

Employers can begin addressing systemic barriers by conducting a diversity audit of their organization. This process involves collecting data on workforce demographics, assessing the diversity of hiring and promotion practices, and identifying areas where employees from diverse backgrounds may face barriers. By evaluating these aspects, employers can pinpoint where improvements in diversity and inclusion efforts are necessary.

Identifying and Eliminating Bias

Using the anti-oppression framework, employers can identify and eliminate bias in their hiring and promotion practices. Strategies for mitigating bias include implementing blind resume screening, assembling diverse interview panels, and providing unconscious bias training to hiring managers and supervisors. These measures can help create a more equitable environment for candidates and employees from all backgrounds.

Establishing Diversity Goals and Targets

To increase the representation of employees from diverse backgrounds, employers can establish diversity goals and targets at all levels of the organization. This may involve setting specific targets for recruiting and promoting employees from underrepresented groups and tracking progress towards these goals over time. By monitoring these metrics, employers can ensure their commitment to diversity remains a priority.

Building Relationships with Diverse Communities

Attracting a diverse pool of candidates can be achieved by building relationships with diverse communities. Employers can partner with community organizations, attend job fairs and events focused on diversity and inclusion, and actively seek out candidates from diverse backgrounds. By engaging with these communities, employers can create a more inclusive talent pipeline and broaden their network.

Providing Support and Resources

To ensure the success of employees from diverse backgrounds, employers can provide support and resources tailored to their needs. This may include mentorship and sponsorship programs, training and development opportunities, and employee resource groups focused on diversity and inclusion. By offering these resources, employers can create an environment where all employees feel supported and empowered to grow within the organization.

By using the anti-oppression framework to identify and address systemic barriers, employers can create a more equitable and inclusive workplace culture that promotes the success and well-being of all employees, regardless of their social identities. This can help to attract and retain diverse talent and build a stronger, more innovative workforce.

Recognize the Intersectionality of Identities

The anti-oppression framework recognizes the ways in which individuals hold multiple social identities that intersect and interact with systems of oppression. Employers can use this framework to understand and address the unique experiences of individuals with intersecting identities, such as women of color or LGBTQ+ individuals with disabilities.

What About Intersectionality?

Conducting a Diversity and Inclusion Assessment

To address the unique experiences of individuals with intersecting identities, employers can begin by conducting a diversity and inclusion assessment. This process involves collecting workforce demographic data and conducting surveys or focus groups to gather employee feedback. By understanding the experiences of employees from different social identities, employers can identify areas where they may face unique barriers.

Using an Intersectional Lens

Employers should use an intersectional lens to recognize the unique experiences of individuals with intersecting identities. This approach acknowledges that individuals hold multiple social identities that interact and intersect with systems of oppression, creating unique experiences of marginalization and discrimination. By considering intersectionality, employers can better understand the complexities of their employees' experiences.

Providing Targeted Support

To address the needs of individuals with intersecting identities, such as women of color or LGBTQ+ individuals with disabilities, employers can provide targeted support. This may include resources and accommodations like flexible work arrangements, assistive technology, or targeted mentorship and sponsorship programs. By offering tailored support, employers can help ensure these employees thrive in the workplace.

Establishing an Inclusive Culture

Creating an inclusive culture that values diversity and recognizes the unique experiences of individuals with intersecting identities is crucial for employers. This can be achieved through implementing policies and practices that promote diversity and inclusion, such as implicit bias training, diversity and inclusion committees, or employee resource groups focused on intersectionality. By fostering an inclusive culture, employers can support the well-being and success of all employees.

Creating Brave Spaces

Employers can also create brave spaces for employees with intersecting identities, allowing them to connect, share experiences, and advocate for their needs and rights. This may involve establishing affinity groups or support networks focused on specific intersections of identities, like a woman of color group or an LGBTQ+ disability group. By offering these spaces, employers can facilitate open dialogue and encourage a more equitable and inclusive workplace culture.

By using the anti-oppression framework to address the unique experiences of individuals with intersecting identities, employers can create a more equitable and inclusive workplace culture that promotes the success and well-being of all employees. This can help to attract and retain diverse talent and build a stronger, more innovative workforce.

Center the Voices of Marginalized Individuals

Employers can use the anti-oppression framework to emphasize the voices and experiences of marginalized individuals in their diversity and inclusion initiatives. Actively seeking input and feedback from diverse backgrounds and incorporating this feedback into policies and practices can lead to a more inclusive work environment.

Conducting Focus Groups and Surveys

To gather input and feedback, employers can conduct focus groups and surveys with employees from diverse backgrounds. These discussions can provide insights into experiences of discrimination, harassment, or exclusion, and generate suggestions for improving workplace culture.

Forming an Employee Diversity Council

Creating an employee diversity council comprised of diverse individuals can facilitate ongoing input and feedback on workplace policies and practices. Empowering the council to make recommendations to senior leadership and holding the organization accountable for implementing diversity and inclusion initiatives can be instrumental in fostering an inclusive environment.

Ensuring Diversity in Leadership

Promoting diversity in leadership by hiring and promoting individuals from diverse backgrounds can help ensure marginalized voices are represented at the highest levels of the organization. Diverse leadership can contribute to more inclusive decision-making processes and policies.

Establishing Inclusion as a Core Value

By making inclusion a core value and prioritizing diversity in all aspects of the business, employers can demonstrate their commitment to creating an equitable workplace. Incorporating diversity and inclusion goals into the organization's strategic plan and tracking progress towards these goals over time can help maintain this focus.

Taking Action on Feedback

Employers should take action on feedback received from diverse employees by implementing policies and practices addressing concerns and suggestions. This may involve revising recruitment and hiring practices, providing training and education on diversity and inclusion, and implementing policies addressing discrimination and harassment in the workplace.

By centering the voices and experiences of marginalized individuals, employers can create a more equitable and inclusive workplace culture that promotes success and well-being for all employees. This approach can attract and retain diverse talent, ultimately leading to a stronger, more innovative workforce.

Challenge Dominant Narratives

The anti-oppression framework helps employers challenge dominant narratives that reinforce systems of oppression and privilege. By using this framework, employers can address their biases, assumptions, and actively promote and celebrate diversity in the workplace.

Conducting Implicit Bias Training

Employers can provide implicit bias training for all employees, helping them recognize and challenge personal biases and assumptions. This training can include education on how bias and discrimination manifest in the workplace and offer tools and strategies for addressing and combating biases.

Promoting Diversity in Communication

Inclusive language and diverse perspectives should be promoted in company communications, such as newsletters and social media. Employers can also celebrate holidays and events significant to employees from diverse backgrounds, fostering an inclusive environment.

Creating Opportunities for Cultural Exchange

Sponsoring cultural events and encouraging employees to share their cultural traditions and experiences allows for cultural exchange and understanding. These opportunities can promote appreciation for diverse cultures and contribute to a more inclusive workplace culture.

Establishing a Diversity and Inclusion Committee

Forming a diversity and inclusion committee consisting of diverse individuals can provide ongoing input and feedback on workplace policies and practices. Empowering the committee to make recommendations to senior leadership and holding the organization accountable for implementing diversity and inclusion initiatives are essential steps in this process.

Celebrating Diversity and Promoting Inclusion

Recognizing and celebrating the contributions of employees from diverse backgrounds through awards, promotions, or public recognition can help create an inclusive workplace culture. By valuing and celebrating diversity, employers can foster an environment where everyone feels supported.

By challenging dominant narratives and promoting diversity in the workplace, employers can create a more equitable and inclusive workplace culture that promotes the success and well-being of all employees. This approach can help attract and retain diverse talent, leading to a stronger, more innovative workforce.

Provide Resources and Support

Employers can utilize the anti-oppression framework to provide resources and support to individuals from marginalized communities. This can be achieved through mentorship and sponsorship programs, training and development opportunities, and employee resource groups.

Offering Mentorship and Sponsorship Programs

Mentorship and sponsorship programs can be offered to employees from marginalized communities, helping them develop relationships with senior leaders and gain access to career opportunities and resources. Pairing employees with experienced mentors or sponsors and providing training and support to both parties can foster growth and development.

Providing Training and Development Opportunities

Offering training and development opportunities to employees from marginalized communities can help them acquire new skills and competencies valued in the workplace. Access to education and training programs, such as leadership development courses or technical training programs, can contribute to their professional growth.

Establishing Employee Resource Groups

Employee resource groups (ERGs) focused on specific communities, like women of color or LGBTQ+ individuals, provide safe and supportive spaces for employees from marginalized communities. ERGs allow employees to connect, share experiences, and advocate for their needs and rights.

Offering Flexible Work Arrangements

Flexible work arrangements can be provided to employees from marginalized communities, helping them balance work and personal responsibilities. Remote work options, flexible hours, or job sharing opportunities can create a more inclusive work environment.

Providing Mental Health Resources

Employers can support the well-being of employees from marginalized communities by offering mental health resources. This may include access to counseling services, mental health days, or resources and training on stress management and self-care.

By offering resources and support to marginalized employees, employers can promote equity and social justice in the workplace, fostering a more inclusive and supportive culture. This approach can attract and retain diverse talent, leading to a stronger, more innovative workforce.

By applying the anti-oppression framework, employers can create a more equitable and inclusive workplace culture that values diversity and promotes the success and well-being of all employees, regardless of their social identities.

Key Questions

What is the purpose of conducting implicit bias training in the workplace?

The purpose of conducting implicit bias training in the workplace is to help employees recognize and challenge personal biases and assumptions. This training can educate employees on how bias and discrimination manifest in the workplace and offer tools and strategies for addressing and combating biases

How can employers promote diversity in communication?

Employers can promote diversity in communication by using inclusive language and incorporating diverse perspectives in company communications, such as newsletters and social media. They can also celebrate holidays and events significant to employees from diverse backgrounds, fostering an inclusive environment.

What is the role of a diversity and inclusion committee in an organization?

The role of a diversity and inclusion committee is to provide ongoing input and feedback on workplace policies and practices related to diversity and inclusion. The committee, consisting of diverse individuals, can make recommendations to senior leadership and hold the organization accountable for implementing diversity and inclusion initiatives.

What are some resources and support employers can provide to individuals from marginalized communities?

Employers can provide resources and support such as mentorship and sponsorship programs, training and development opportunities, employee resource groups, flexible work arrangements, and mental health resources. These resources can contribute to professional growth, create a more inclusive work environment, and support the well-being of employees from marginalized communities.

How can applying the anti-oppression framework benefit the workplace?

By applying the anti-oppression framework, employers can create a more equitable and inclusive workplace culture that values diversity and promotes the success and well-being of all employees, regardless of their social identities. This approach can help attract and retain diverse talent, leading to a stronger, more innovative workforce.

How can employers create opportunities for cultural exchange within the workplace?

Employers can create opportunities for cultural exchange by sponsoring cultural events and encouraging employees to share their cultural traditions and experiences. These opportunities promote appreciation for diverse cultures and contribute to a more inclusive workplace culture.

How can establishing employee resource groups (ERGs) benefit employees from marginalized communities?

Establishing employee resource groups (ERGs) focused on specific communities, such as women of color or LGBTQ+ individuals, provides safe and supportive spaces for employees from marginalized communities. ERGs allow employees to connect, share experiences, and advocate for their needs and rights, fostering a more inclusive work environment.

How can the anti-oppression framework help employers in addressing systemic barriers in the workplace?

The anti-oppression framework can help employers identify and address systemic barriers that prevent individuals from diverse backgrounds from entering and succeeding in the workforce. This can include barriers related to hiring practices, promotion, and retention. Employers can use this framework to evaluate diversity in their organization, implement unbiased practices, establish diversity goals, build relationships with diverse communities, and provide tailored support and resources.

What are the key principles of the Intersectional Anti-Oppression Framework?

The key principles of the Intersectional Anti-Oppression Framework include recognizing the interconnected nature of social identities and systems of oppression, addressing unique experiences of oppression and marginalization, promoting equity and social justice, centering the voices and experiences of marginalized individuals and communities, and recognizing and challenging dominant narratives and structures that reinforce systems of oppression.

How can employers use the anti-oppression framework to support employees with intersecting identities?

Employers can use the anti-oppression framework to understand and address the unique experiences of individuals with intersecting identities, such as women of color or LGBTQ+ individuals with disabilities. By recognizing these intersections, employers can create tailored resources and support systems, ensuring a more inclusive and equitable work environment for all employees.

Practice 4.1

Role Play Scenario
Reach Pull Push Inc.'s Anti-Oppression Framework Implementation

Roles
1. CEO of Reach Pull Push Inc..
2. Human Resources Manager
3. Employee from a marginalized community
4. Employee from a non-marginalized community
5. Employee Resource Group (ERG) leader

Scene
A company-wide meeting has been called to discuss the implementation and progress of Reach Pull Push Inc.'s anti-oppression framework.

CEO
(Opening the meeting) Thank you all for joining today's meeting. As you know, we've been working hard to implement an anti-oppression framework here at Reach Pull Push Inc.. We recognize the importance of addressing systemic barriers and discrimination faced by marginalized communities. Our aim is to create a supportive and inclusive workplace culture that promotes equity and social justice. I would like to invite our Human Resources Manager to share some of the initiatives we have implemented.

Human Resources Manager
Thank you, CEO. We have made several changes in our hiring practices to attract diverse candidates, such as using inclusive job descriptions and implementing blind resume screening. We have also established policies to promote equity in compensation, ensuring that all employees receive equitable and comparable salaries. Additionally, we have implemented mentorship and sponsorship programs, as well as professional development opportunities for employees from marginalized communities.

Employee from a marginalized community

I appreciate the efforts that have been made so far. The mentorship program has been particularly helpful for me in building connections with senior leaders. However, I think there is still room for improvement in addressing microaggressions and fostering a more inclusive company culture.

Employee from a non-marginalized community: I've noticed positive changes in the workplace since we started implementing the anti-oppression framework, but I'm still learning how to be a better ally. Are there any resources or training available to help us better understand and support our colleagues from marginalized communities?

1. What specific steps has the Human Resources department taken to ensure that job descriptions are inclusive and unbiased?
2. How does the company measure the success of its blind resume screening process in promoting diverse hiring?
3. What are possible examples cCan the Employee from a marginalized community provide of microaggressions they have experienced or witnessed in the workplace, and suggest ways the company could address these issues?
4. What initiatives has the company implemented to promote allyship among employees from non-marginalized communities, and how can these initiatives be improved or expanded?
5. As an ERG leader, what challenges have you faced in engaging employees from non-marginalized communities, and how do you plan to overcome these challenges?
6. How does the company plan to monitor and evaluate the effectiveness of its mentorship and sponsorship programs in supporting employees from marginalized communities?
7. What steps has the company taken to ensure that employees are aware of and have access to professional development opportunities specifically designed for marginalized communities?

INTERSECTIONAL LEADERSHIP: BUILDING RESILIENT WORKFORCES

8. How does Reach Pull Push Inc.. plan to continue to evolve its anti-oppression framework to stay proactive and responsive to the needs and experiences of employees from marginalized communities?

9. What are the short-term and long-term goals of the company's diversity and inclusion initiatives, and how will progress towards these goals be tracked and communicated to employees?

10. How can employees from both marginalized and non-marginalized communities contribute to creating a more inclusive and supportive workplace culture, and what resources or support can the company provide to facilitate this process?

Practice 4.2

Group Activity
Understanding and Applying the Intersectional Anti-Oppression Framework in the Workplace

Objective
To help participants understand the Intersectional Anti-Oppression Framework and learn how to apply it in their workplace to promote equity, diversity, and inclusion.

Materials
1. Flipchart or whiteboard for brainstorming and note-taking.
2. Markers or pens for writing.
3. Handout with a brief overview of the Intersectional Anti-Oppression Framework (optional).

Instructions
1. Begin by providing a brief introduction to the Intersectional Anti-Oppression Framework and its key principles. Distribute the handout if you have one prepared.
2. Divide participants into small groups of 4-5 people.
3. Instruct each group to discuss the importance of recognizing and addressing the interconnected nature of social identities and systems of oppression in the workplace.
4. Ask each group to consider the ways in which their organization can identify and address systemic barriers that prevent individuals from diverse backgrounds from entering and succeeding in the workforce. Encourage them to brainstorm strategies for conducting a diversity audit, identifying and eliminating bias, and establishing diversity goals and targets.

Instructions (cont.)

5. Have each group discuss strategies for building relationships with diverse communities and attracting a diverse pool of candidates. Encourage them to think about potential partnerships with community organizations, job fairs, and events focused on diversity and inclusion.

6. Instruct groups to explore strategies for providing support and resources tailored to the needs of employees from diverse backgrounds, such as mentorship programs, training and development opportunities, and employee resource groups.

7. After the small group discussions, reconvene as a larger group and have each team present their findings and strategies. Facilitate a group discussion on the importance of applying the Intersectional Anti-Oppression Framework in the workplace and how it can contribute to a more inclusive and equitable environment.

8. Encourage participants to reflect on the following questions:
    - How can you apply the Intersectional Anti-Oppression Framework in your workplace to address systemic barriers and promote equity?
    - What steps can you take to ensure that employees from diverse backgrounds feel seen, valued, and supported in your organization?
    - How can you create opportunities for professional development and growth for employees with intersecting identities?

9. Conclude the activity by summarizing the key takeaways and encouraging participants to implement the strategies discussed in their workplace to create a more inclusive and equitable environment for all employees, regardless of their social identities.

LEVELING: EQUITY & JUSTICE

Answer Key 4.1

1. To ensure job descriptions are inclusive and unbiased, the Human Resources department has consulted with diversity experts, removed gender-specific language, focused on essential skills and qualifications, and avoided using exclusionary requirements or jargon.

2. The company measures the success of its blind resume screening process by tracking the demographics of candidates advancing to the interview stage, and ultimately, monitoring the diversity of new hires over time.

3. Examples of microaggressions experienced by the Employee from a marginalized community include coworkers making assumptions about their background or qualifications, insensitive comments, and being excluded from social events. The company could address these issues through awareness training, open discussions, and clear policies against discrimination.

4. The company has implemented initiatives such as allyship workshops, unconscious bias training, and inclusive language guides. These initiatives can be improved by offering ongoing training, encouraging active participation, and providing opportunities for employees to engage with marginalized colleagues in meaningful ways.

5. As an ERG leader, challenges faced in engaging employees from non-marginalized communities include lack of awareness and understanding of ERGs' purpose, and reluctance to participate due to fear of saying or doing the wrong thing. Overcoming these challenges may involve promoting the benefits of ERGs to all employees, providing clear expectations for allyship, and creating opportunities for open dialogue.

6. The company plans to monitor and evaluate the effectiveness of its mentorship and sponsorship programs by collecting feedback from participants, tracking career progress and retention rates of mentees, and adjusting the programs based on outcomes and evolving needs.

7. To ensure employees are aware of and have access to professional development opportunities, the company has shared information through various channels, such as company newsletters, intranet, and ERG meetings. Additionally, the company has allocated a specific budget for these opportunities to ensure accessibility.

8. Reach Pull Push Inc.. plans to continue evolving its anti-oppression framework by regularly reviewing and updating policies, soliciting feedback from employees, staying informed on best practices, and responding to changes in the workforce and broader society.

9. The short-term and long-term goals of the company's diversity and inclusion initiatives include increasing the representation of marginalized employees at all levels, fostering an inclusive culture, and reducing instances of discrimination. Progress towards these goals will be tracked using key performance indicators and communicated through annual diversity reports and regular updates.

10. Employees from both marginalized and non-marginalized communities can contribute to a more inclusive and supportive workplace culture by actively participating in ERGs, attending training sessions, engaging in open dialogue, and challenging biases. The company can facilitate this process by providing resources, support, and a safe environment for open discussion and learning.

"She/Her"

Dear Boss,

I am writing to bring your attention to a situation that has been causing me considerable distress at work. I have been experiencing repeated instances of inappropriate sexist behavior and refusal to use my preferred pronoun by a fellow employee, Barb. As you know, I identify as female, and my preferred pronouns are she/her.

Over the past few weeks, Barb has consistently refused to address me by my preferred pronouns, despite my multiple attempts to politely correct them and explain the importance of using the correct pronouns. This refusal has made me feel disrespected and uncomfortable in my workplace. Additionally, Barb has exhibited inappropriate sexist behavior on several occasions, including making derogatory comments about my gender, which has further contributed to a hostile work environment.

I understand that Reach NPO is committed to promoting diversity and inclusion, and I believe that addressing this issue is crucial to maintaining a respectful and inclusive work environment for all employees.

I kindly request that you address this matter promptly and take appropriate action to ensure that Barb understands the importance of respecting their colleagues' gender identities and refrains from engaging in sexist behavior. I am confident that with your support and intervention, we can resolve this issue and foster a more inclusive and respectful work environment.

Sincerely,
Sammy She/Her

Chapter 5
Feminist Framework

Current statistics show that women and those who identify with she/her pronouns remain underrepresented in leadership positions in many industries and countries around the world. While progress has been made in recent years, there is still a significant gender gap in leadership.

A Note about Pronouns

When discussing individuals who use the pronouns she/her, it's important to recognize the significance of using correct pronouns in the workplace. Inclusivity and respect are promoted through the appropriate use of pronouns, contributing to a sense of belonging for all employees, including those who are transgender or non-binary. The use of pronouns in the workplace is an important aspect of fostering an inclusive and respectful work environment.

Recent statistics on women in leadership positions:

1. Women make up only 10% of Fortune 500 CEOs (Fortune, 2023).

2. Only 28.5% of school district superintendents are women (Zippia, 2022).

3. Only 25% of senior management positions globally are held by women (Grant Thornton, 2021).

4. Women hold just 28% of managerial positions in the United States (U.S. Bureau of Labor Statistics, 2021).

5. Women make up only 22.5% of members of parliament worldwide (Inter-Parliamentary Union, 2021).

6. Women hold just 6.6% of CEO positions in the S&P 500 (Catalyst, 2021).

These statistics demonstrate that there is still a significant gender gap in leadership positions across industries and countries. While progress has been made in recent years, more work needs to be done to promote gender equity in leadership and to create more opportunities for women to succeed and advance in their careers.

A feminist framework is a way of thinking and analyzing the world through a lens that prioritizes gender equality and challenges gender-based discrimination and oppression. It is an approach that recognizes the systemic power imbalances that exist between men and women, and seeks to address these imbalances through activism, policy-making, and social change.

Feminist thought can be traced back to early writings by women such as Mary Wollstonecraft and her work "A Vindication of the Rights of Woman" (1792), but it has significantly evolved since then.

Feminism is often divided into various waves, with each wave addressing different aspects of gender inequality and women's rights. Here are some key figures from each wave:

1. First-wave feminism (late 19th to early 20th century): This wave primarily focused on women's suffrage, the right to vote, and other legal rights. Key figures include Susan B. Anthony, Elizabeth Cady Stanton, and Lucretia Mott.

2. Second-wave feminism (1960s-1980s): This wave broadened its focus to include issues such as reproductive rights, workplace equality, and sexual liberation. Key figures include Betty Friedan, Gloria Steinem, and bell hooks.

3. Third-wave feminism (1990s-present): This wave is characterized by its emphasis on intersectionality, recognizing that women's experiences of oppression are shaped by factors such as race, class, and sexual orientation. Key figures include Kimberlé Crenshaw, who coined the term "intersectionality," as well as Rebecca Walker and Judith Butler.

Feminism is a continually evolving field, with new perspectives and ideas emerging as society changes and progresses. Feminist frameworks are based on the idea that gender is not just a biological fact, but a socially constructed identity that is shaped by cultural norms and expectations. Feminist frameworks challenge traditional gender roles and stereotypes, and seek to promote gender equity by advocating for the rights of women and other marginalized gender identities.

Feminist frameworks are used across a range of disciplines, including sociology, political science, psychology, and literature. They are also commonly used in activism and advocacy work, as well as in policy-making and program development aimed at addressing gender-based discrimination and violence.

The feminist framework can have a significant impact on hiring practices, particularly in terms of promoting gender equality and addressing gender-based discrimination in the workplace.

Challenging gender roles at work means actively questioning and working to change traditional gender-based assumptions and expectations that may influence how people are perceived and treated in the workplace based on their gender.

Historically, many professions and industries have been dominated by one gender or the other, with certain jobs or tasks being associated with masculinity or femininity. Challenging gender roles at work involves recognizing and challenging these assumptions, and actively working to create a more equitable and inclusive workplace.

Perspectives on female bosses can vary widely depending on cultural, social, and individual factors. Historically, women have faced significant barriers to leadership roles, and gender stereotypes and biases can still impact how female identifying bosses are perceived and evaluated in the workplace.

Many people have a positive view of female bosses, and believe that women can be just as effective, capable, and successful as male bosses. Female bosses are often praised for their communication skills, emotional intelligence, and ability to build strong relationships with their employees.

Unfortunately, some people hold negative stereotypes and biases about female bosses, and may view them as less competent, less authoritative, or less effective than male bosses. Some people may view female bosses as overly emotional, or as lacking the assertiveness and confidence needed to succeed in a leadership role.

Some people may not hold strong opinions about female bosses one way or the other, and may judge them based on their individual skills, abilities, and leadership style. It is important to recognize that perspectives on female bosses can be influenced by a range of factors, including gender stereotypes, cultural norms, and personal experiences.

While progress has been made in recent years to promote gender equity in leadership roles, there is still work to be done to address bias and ensure that all employees, regardless of gender, have equal opportunities to succeed and advance in the workplace. Attracting more female leaders necessitates a proactive strategy to identify and engage qualified female candidates for leadership roles.

Hiring Process

Examine your existing hiring process to uncover any potential biases or obstacles that may prevent female candidates from applying or progressing through the recruitment stages. For instance, ensure your job descriptions are gender-neutral and that your hiring team is trained to recognize and address any gender-based stereotypes or biases.

Prioritize Diversity

Emphasize diversity in your recruitment efforts by actively seeking and advertising job openings to a diverse pool of candidates, including women. Consider collaborating with organizations that support women in leadership roles, such as women's professional associations, and participating in career fairs aimed at diverse candidates.

Create a Supportive Workplace Culture

Cultivating a supportive workplace culture that values and fosters diversity can help attract and retain female leaders. This could involve implementing policies and practices that encourage work-life balance, offering mentorship and leadership training programs, and providing opportunities for employees to give feedback and propose improvements.

Focus on Development and Advancement

Offer opportunities for female employees to enhance their skills and further their careers within your organization. This could include providing leadership development programs, establishing a mentorship program for female employees, or implementing a system to track and acknowledge employee contributions and accomplishments.

Monitor and Evaluate Progress

Consistently monitor and assess your recruitment and retention efforts to gauge the effectiveness of your diversity initiatives. This could involve tracking the number of female candidates who apply for leadership positions and monitoring the retention rates of female employees in leadership roles.

Recruiting more female leaders demands a proactive and deliberate approach that emphasizes diversity and equity in the workplace. By establishing a supportive workplace culture and providing opportunities for growth and advancement, you can attract and retain talented she/her leaders who can contribute to your organization's success and growth.

EQUAL PAY

Economic Justice

Equal pay is a matter of economic justice, as it ensures that all workers are paid fairly for their work, regardless of their gender. Women have historically been paid less than men for doing the same job, which perpetuates economic inequality and limits their opportunities for financial stability and upward mobility.

Gender Equality

Equal pay is a critical component of gender equality, as it helps to eliminate gender-based discrimination and bias in the workplace. When women are paid less than men for the same job, it sends a message that their work is less valuable than men's work, which can lead to a range of negative consequences, including reduced confidence, lower self-esteem, and limited opportunities for career advancement.

Talent Retention

Equal pay is also important for talent retention, as it helps to attract and retain top talent, regardless of gender. When organizations prioritize equal pay and demonstrate a commitment to gender equity, they are more likely to attract and retain skilled employees who are looking for a workplace that values and supports them.

Economic Growth

Equal pay can also contribute to overall economic growth, as it ensures that workers are paid based on their skills and contributions, rather than their gender. When workers are paid fairly for their work, they are more likely to be motivated, productive, and engaged, which can lead to increased innovation and improved business outcomes.

Overall, equal pay is important because it ensures that all workers are treated fairly and equitably, regardless of their gender. By eliminating gender-based discrimination and bias in the workplace, organizations can create a more inclusive and supportive work environment that benefits everyone.

Addressing Discrimination and Harassment

Legal Measures

Legal measures can help to protect women from discrimination and harassment in the workplace. This might include policies and regulations that prohibit gender-based discrimination and harassment, and provide mechanisms for reporting and investigating incidents of discrimination and harassment.

Organizational Policies

Organizations can implement policies and procedures that promote a safe and respectful workplace environment. This might include anti-discrimination and anti-harassment policies, training programs for employees and managers on recognizing and preventing discrimination and harassment, and providing clear reporting and investigation procedures for incidents of discrimination and harassment.

Cultural Change

Addressing discrimination and harassment against women also requires a cultural shift that challenges gender-based stereotypes and biases. This might involve creating a workplace culture that values and promotes diversity and inclusion, providing opportunities for women to participate in leadership and decision-making roles, and addressing unconscious bias through training and education.

Support Systems

Organizations can also implement support systems for employees who have experienced discrimination or harassment. This might include employee assistance programs, counseling services, and support groups for employees who have experienced discrimination or harassment.

Accountability

It is important to hold perpetrators of discrimination and harassment accountable for their actions. This might involve disciplinary action, including termination of employment, for employees who engage in discriminatory or harassing behavior

Develop and Enforce Policies

Develop clear policies and procedures that prohibit discrimination and harassment based on gender, and ensure that all employees are trained on these policies. Hold all employees, including managers and supervisors, accountable for violating these policies.

Provide Training and Education

Provide training and education to employees on topics related to gender equity, unconscious bias, and sexual harassment prevention. This can help to create a more inclusive workplace culture that values diversity and supports all employees.

Create Reporting Channels

Create clear and accessible channels for employees to report incidents of discrimination or harassment. Ensure that employees feel safe and supported when making a report, and that all reports are taken seriously and investigated promptly.

Offer Support to Victims

Offer support and resources to employees who have experienced discrimination or harassment, including counseling, legal advice, and other forms of support. Ensure that employees are aware of these resources and how to access them.

Foster a Culture of Respect

Foster a culture of respect and civility in the workplace, and encourage employees to speak up if they witness or experience any form of discrimination or harassment. Ensure that all employees are treated with respect and dignity, and that everyone feels valued and supported.

Regularly Review and Assess Progress

Regularly review and assess progress in addressing discrimination and harassment against women in the workplace. Monitor employee feedback, conduct regular surveys, and review data on promotion rates, salaries, and other metrics to identify areas for improvement.

By implementing these strategies, organizations can create a more inclusive and supportive workplace culture that values and supports all employees, regardless of their gender. This can help to promote gender equity, reduce discrimination and harassment, and create a more productive and successful organization.

Overall, addressing discrimination and harassment against women requires a commitment to creating a safe, inclusive, and respectful workplace environment. By implementing legal, organizational, and cultural strategies that promote gender equity and support women in the workplace, organizations can create a more positive and productive workplace environment for all employees.

PROMOTE WOMEN IN THE WORKFORCE

Mentor and sponsor women

Mentor and sponsor women by offering guidance, advice, and support to help them develop their skills, build their confidence, and advance their careers. Be an advocate for their professional development and help them connect with key people in your network.

Create opportunities

Create opportunities for women to take on leadership roles and gain new experiences. Provide them with challenging assignments, stretch goals, and opportunities to lead high-impact projects.

Challenge gender bias

Challenge gender bias in the workplace by calling out instances of discrimination, bias, or sexism that you observe or experience. Encourage others to do the same and promote a culture of inclusion and respect.

Support work-life balance

Support work-life balance by offering flexible work arrangements, such as telecommuting or flexible hours, to help women balance their work and personal responsibilities.

Provide equal opportunities

Ensure that women have equal opportunities for training, development, and promotion. Ensure that performance evaluations and promotions are based on objective criteria and that gender bias is eliminated.

Advocate for equal pay

Advocate for equal pay for women by ensuring that women are paid fairly and equitably for their work. Conduct regular pay equity audits to identify and address any pay disparities that exist.

Participate in women's networks

Participate in women's networks and support groups to help build relationships with other women in the workplace and provide a supportive community.

By taking these actions, you can help promote women in the workforce and create a more inclusive and supportive workplace culture that values and supports diversity and gender equity.

Key Questions

What are some strategies that organizations can use to attract and engage qualified female candidates for leadership roles?

Organizations can attract and engage qualified female candidates for leadership roles by implementing inclusive hiring practices, providing targeted development and mentorship programs, showcasing female role models in leadership, offering flexible work arrangements, and fostering a supportive and inclusive work culture that values diversity and gender equity.

How can organizations address the negative stereotypes and biases about female bosses to promote a more equitable workplace?

Organizations can address negative stereotypes and biases about female bosses by providing training and education on unconscious bias and gender equity, promoting open dialogue about gender stereotypes, showcasing positive examples of female leadership, and implementing policies and practices that support the advancement and success of women in leadership roles.

What role can male allies play in promoting gender equity in leadership and supporting female colleagues in the workplace?

Male allies can play a crucial role in promoting gender equity in leadership by actively supporting and advocating for their female colleagues, challenging gender stereotypes and biases, participating in diversity and inclusion initiatives, and using their influence and positions of power to create opportunities for women and other underrepresented groups in the workplace.

How can feminist frameworks be applied to address the gender gap in leadership across different industries and countries?

Feminist frameworks can be applied to address the gender gap in leadership across different industries and countries by advocating for gender-responsive policies and legislation, raising awareness about gender-based discrimination and inequality, promoting intersectional approaches to gender equity, and engaging in activism and advocacy to challenge systemic barriers that hinder women's advancement in leadership roles.

What are the potential benefits of having a more diverse and gender-balanced leadership team in an organization?

The potential benefits of having a more diverse and gender-balanced leadership team include increased creativity and innovation, improved decision-making, better problem-solving, enhanced employee engagement, higher retention rates, improved financial performance, and a more positive organizational reputation and brand image.

How can organizations foster a culture of allyship and support for women and marginalized gender identities in the workplace?

Organizations can foster a culture of allyship and support for women and marginalized gender identities by providing training and resources on diversity and inclusion, establishing employee resource groups, promoting open communication and dialogue about issues related to gender equity, and implementing policies and practices that support a safe, inclusive, and respectful work environment for all employees.

How can organizations ensure that their diversity and inclusion efforts are intersectional and take into account the unique challenges faced by women from diverse backgrounds (e.g., women of color, LGBTQ+ women, women with disabilities)?

Organizations can ensure that their diversity and inclusion efforts are intersectional by adopting an inclusive approach that recognizes and addresses the unique challenges faced by women from diverse backgrounds. This can be achieved by providing targeted support and resources, engaging diverse voices in decision-making processes, addressing systemic barriers to inclusion, and monitoring progress to ensure that diversity initiatives are effectively addressing the needs of all employees.

Key Questions (cont.)

What role can human resources and talent management teams play in promoting gender equity in the workplace and addressing the gender gap in leadership?

Human resources and talent management teams can play a pivotal role in promoting gender equity in the workplace and addressing the gender gap in leadership by implementing inclusive hiring and promotion practices, developing targeted leadership development and mentorship programs, providing training on unconscious bias and diversity, monitoring progress towards gender equity goals, and fostering a supportive and inclusive work culture that values diversity and equal opportunities for all employees.

She/Her: Feminist Framework

Practice 5.1

Company X is a mid-sized organization that has recently acknowledged the need for greater gender diversity in its leadership. The company's executive team is currently composed of 80% men and 20% women. Company X decides to create and implement a new initiative to increase the number of women in leadership positions within the organization. The company wants to ensure that the initiative is guided by feminist principles and effectively addresses gender-based discrimination and inequality in the workplace.

Questions to analyze the scenario through a feminist framework:

1. How can Company X challenge and deconstruct existing gender stereotypes and biases that may be influencing the perception of women in leadership roles within the organization?
2. How can the organization ensure that its hiring and promotion practices are equitable and do not unfairly favor male candidates for leadership positions?
3. How can Company X create a more inclusive and supportive work environment that encourages and values the contributions of women and other marginalized gender identities?
4. What can Company X do to address potential intersectional barriers that women from diverse backgrounds (e.g., women of color, LGBTQ+ women, women with disabilities) may face in accessing leadership opportunities within the organization?
5. How can Company X involve existing female leaders in the process of designing and implementing the new initiative, ensuring that their voices and perspectives are heard and valued?
6. What training or educational resources can Company X provide to its employees to promote awareness of gender biases, stereotypes, and the importance of gender equity in the workplace?
7. How can Company X measure the success of the initiative and ensure that progress towards greater gender diversity in leadership is sustained and continually improved over time?

Practice 5.2

Group Activity
Equal Pay Workshop

Objective
To educate employees on the importance of equal pay, raise awareness about gender pay disparities, and promote actions for achieving equal pay in the workplace.

Materials Needed
1. Whiteboard or flip chart
2. Markers
3. Handouts on equal pay statistics and relevant legislation
4. Case studies or real-life examples of pay disparities
5. Laptop and projector for presentations (optional)

Duration
2 Hours

Agenda
1. Introduction (10 minutes)
   - Welcome participants and explain the objectives of the workshop.
   - Introduce the facilitators and provide a brief overview of the agenda.
2. Presentation: The Importance of Equal Pay (20 minutes)
   - Share statistics and facts about the gender pay gap and its impact on individuals, organizations, and society.
   - Discuss the legal and ethical aspects of equal pay.
   - Explain the benefits of equal pay, including talent retention, economic growth, and gender equality.
3. Small Group Discussions: Identifying Pay Disparities (30 minutes)
   - Divide participants into small groups.
   - Provide each group with a case study or real-life example of pay disparities.
   - Ask groups to discuss the example and identify the underlying causes of the pay gap.

- Encourage participants to share their own experiences or observations of pay disparities in the workplace.

4. Large Group Discussion: Strategies for Achieving Equal Pay (40 minutes)
   - Reconvene as a large group and ask each small group to share their findings and insights from the previous discussion.
   - Facilitate a large group discussion on strategies for achieving equal pay in the workplace, including:
     - Developing and enforcing policies on equal pay
     - Conducting regular pay audits and assessments
     - Providing training and education on unconscious bias and gender equity
     - Establishing transparent and merit-based compensation practices
     - Encouraging open dialogue and communication about pay

5. Action Planning (20 minutes)
   - Ask participants to individually create a list of actions they can take in their roles to promote equal pay in the workplace.
   - Encourage participants to consider actions at different levels, such as personal, team, and organizational levels.
   - Invite volunteers to share their action plans with the group.

6. Conclusion and Next Steps (10 minutes)
   - Summarize the key insights and learnings from the workshop.
   - Discuss potential next steps for the organization to continue working towards equal pay, such as scheduling follow-up workshops, conducting pay audits, or establishing a diversity and inclusion committee.
   - Thank participants for their engagement and contributions to the workshop.

Intersectional Leadership: Building Resilient Workforces

Answer Key 5.1

1. Company X can challenge and deconstruct existing gender stereotypes and biases by offering training and workshops that address unconscious bias, conducting regular reviews of company policies and practices to identify and eliminate gendered language, and promoting positive examples of women in leadership roles both within and outside the organization. Encouraging open conversations about gender biases and stereotypes can also help create a more inclusive and equitable work environment.

2. The organization can ensure equitable hiring and promotion practices by implementing blind recruitment processes, standardizing job descriptions and requirements, using diverse interview panels, and setting diversity targets or quotas for leadership positions. Regular audits of hiring and promotion data can also help identify potential disparities and inform adjustments to the process.

3. Company X can create a more inclusive work environment by offering flexible work arrangements, establishing mentorship and sponsorship programs, providing resources and support for employees with caregiving responsibilities, and celebrating the achievements of women and marginalized gender identities within the organization. Implementing inclusive policies and practices, such as gender-neutral restrooms and inclusive language in communication, can also contribute to a more supportive work environment.

4. Company X can address intersectional barriers by implementing diversity and inclusion training that emphasizes intersectionality, providing targeted mentorship and development opportunities for underrepresented groups, and ensuring that diversity initiatives consider the unique needs and experiences of women from diverse backgrounds. Actively seeking feedback from these groups and involving them in decision-making processes can also help address intersectional barriers.

5. Company X can involve existing female leaders by establishing a gender diversity task force or committee that includes women from various levels of leadership, soliciting input and feedback from female leaders through focus groups or surveys, and incorporating their insights into the design and implementation of the new initiative. Recognizing and celebrating the contributions of female leaders can also help ensure that their voices are valued.

6. Company X can provide training and educational resources such as workshops on unconscious bias, gender equity, and allyship; offering e-learning courses on diversity and inclusion topics; and sharing articles, books, and videos that discuss gender biases, stereotypes, and the importance of gender equity in the workplace. Regularly hosting guest speakers or panel discussions on gender-related topics can also help raise awareness and promote ongoing learning.

7. Company X can measure the success of the initiative by tracking key performance indicators such as the representation of women and other marginalized gender identities in leadership positions, the retention and promotion rates of women, and employee engagement and satisfaction scores related to diversity and inclusion. Regularly reviewing and updating the initiative, incorporating feedback from employees, and benchmarking against industry standards can help ensure sustained progress and continual improvement.

She/Her: Feminist Framework

"I Am"

Dear Boss,

I am writing to discuss a recent situation that has been weighing on my mind, and I believe it's important to share my thoughts and feelings with you. As you may recall, there was a promotion opportunity within our team a few weeks ago, and I chose not to apply for the position. Upon reflection, I have come to realize that the reason behind my decision was the impact of stereotype threat on my confidence and self-perception. I felt like an inappropriate label has been my shadow.

I was concerned that my application for the promotion might inadvertently reinforce negative stereotypes associated with my accent. This fear significantly affected my confidence and led me to doubt my qualifications and abilities, even though I know that I possess the skills and experience necessary to excel in the role.

I feel that not applying for the promotion was a missed opportunity, and I regret not having the confidence to put my name forward. I recognize now that my concerns were rooted in stereotype threat rather than an objective evaluation of my capabilities. In hindsight, I wish I had been more aware of the influence of stereotype threat on my decision-making and had taken steps to overcome it.

Sincerely,
Adam

Chapter 6
Stereotype Threat

Stereotype threat is a psychological phenomenon that occurs when individuals feel at risk of confirming a negative stereotype about their social group. This can lead to anxiety, reduced performance, and disengagement.

The concept of stereotype threat was first introduced by social psychologists Claude Steele and Joshua Aronson in a 1995 paper titled "Stereotype Threat and the Intellectual Test Performance of African Americans". Steele and Aronson defined stereotype threat as "being at risk of confirming, as self-characteristic, a negative stereotype about one's group."

Since then, the concept of stereotype threat has been studied and expanded upon by numerous researchers in various fields, including psychology, sociology, education, and neuroscience.

Stereotypes are social beliefs or expectations about certain groups of people, based on characteristics such as race, gender, age, or sexual orientation. Stereotype threat occurs when individuals feel that their performance or behavior is being judged through the lens of a negative stereotype associated with their social group. This can cause them to experience anxiety or stress, which can interfere with their ability to perform at their best.

For example, a woman who is aware of the stereotype that women are less skilled at math than men may experience stereotype threat when taking a math test. She may feel anxious about the possibility of confirming this stereotype and perform worse on the test as a result.

Stereotype threat can have negative consequences for individuals and organizations. It can lead to reduced performance, disengagement, and attrition among members of stigmatized groups. It can also contribute to a lack of diversity and equity in the workplace.

To mitigate stereotype threat, it is important to create a workplace culture that is inclusive, supportive, and values diversity. Leaders can adopt intersectional leadership practices to promote a sense of belonging and reduce the impact of negative stereotypes. Stereotype threat can impact hiring in several ways. It can influence both the hiring decisions of employers and the job-seeking behaviors of applicants.

Stereotype Threat at Work

For employers, stereotype threat can lead to biased hiring decisions based on negative stereotypes about certain groups of people. For example, an employer may hold the stereotype that women are less competent than men in certain fields, leading them to unconsciously favor male candidates over female candidates during the hiring process.

Stereotype threat can also impact the job-seeking behaviors of applicants from stigmatized groups. For example, individuals who feel at risk of confirming a negative stereotype about their social group may be less likely to apply for jobs that are perceived as being dominated by another group. This can lead to a lack of diversity in the applicant pool and limit the pool of potential hires.

To mitigate the impact of stereotype threat on hiring, it is important for employers to adopt inclusive practices that promote diversity and equity. This can include actively recruiting candidates from underrepresented groups, using inclusive language in job postings, and using diverse hiring panels to evaluate candidates. Employers can also provide training to help mitigate the effects of bias and stereotype threat on the hiring process.

Create a Culture of Inclusion

A culture of inclusion can help reduce the impact of stereotype threat by fostering a sense of belonging and value among all employees. This includes promoting equity and diversity, providing opportunities for employees to connect and build relationships, and ensuring that all employees feel valued and respected.

A culture of inclusion is essential for reducing the impact of stereotype threat and creating a workplace where all employees can thrive. In such a culture, every employee feels valued and included, regardless of their background or identity. By fostering a sense of belonging and value among all employees, leaders can help mitigate the negative effects of stereotype threat and promote a more diverse, equitable, and inclusive workplace.

Promoting equity and diversity is an important part of creating a culture of inclusion. This means recognizing and valuing the unique experiences and perspectives of every employee, and actively working to promote equity and inclusion in all aspects of the workplace. Leaders can do this by implementing policies and practices that promote fairness, such as pay equity, diverse hiring and promotion practices, and anti-discrimination policies. They can also create opportunities for employees to share their experiences and perspectives, such as through employee resource groups, diversity and inclusion committees, and feedback mechanisms.

Providing opportunities for employees to connect and build relationships is also key to creating a culture of inclusion. This can involve team-building activities, social events, and other opportunities for employees to get to know one another and build relationships. When employees feel connected to one another, they are more likely to feel a sense of belonging and support, which can help to mitigate the negative effects of stereotype threat.

Finally, ensuring that all employees feel valued and respected is critical for creating a culture of inclusion. This involves treating every employee with respect and dignity, regardless of their background or identity. It also means recognizing and celebrating the contributions of all employees, and creating a workplace culture where everyone's contributions are valued and recognized.

By creating a culture of inclusion, leaders can help reduce the impact of stereotype threat and create a workplace where all employees feel valued, respected, and empowered to contribute their best work. This can lead to higher employee engagement, retention, and productivity, and ultimately drive better business outcomes.

Provide Resources and Support

Providing resources and support to employees can help to reduce the effects of stereotype threat. This can include coaching, mentorship, or other forms of support that help employees to build confidence and improve their performance.

Providing resources and support is critical for mitigating the effects of stereotype threat and promoting the success of diverse employees. Stereotype threat can lead to reduced performance and disengagement among individuals from stigmatized groups. By providing resources and support, leaders can help employees to build confidence, reduce anxiety, and improve their performance.

Coaching is one form of support that can be particularly effective in mitigating the effects of stereotype threat. Coaching involves providing guidance and support to help employees develop their skills and abilities. This can include providing feedback on performance, identifying areas for improvement, and providing strategies for overcoming challenges.

Mentorship is another effective form of support. Mentors can provide guidance and support to employees, particularly those from underrepresented groups, to help them navigate the workplace and build their careers. Mentors can help employees to build confidence, identify opportunities for growth and development, and provide advice on how to overcome challenges.

Other forms of support can include training, professional development opportunities, and employee resource groups. Training can help employees to develop the skills and knowledge they need to succeed in their roles. Professional development opportunities can provide employees with opportunities to learn and grow, and to develop their careers. Employee resource groups can provide a sense of community and support for employees from underrepresented groups.

By providing resources and support, leaders can help to reduce the effects of stereotype threat and promote the success of diverse employees. This can lead to higher employee engagement, retention, and productivity, and ultimately drive better business outcomes. It is important for leaders to recognize the unique needs and experiences of their employees and to provide customized support that meets those needs.

Address Bias and Discrimination

It's important for leaders to actively address bias and discrimination in the workplace. This includes holding individuals accountable for discriminatory behavior, promoting fairness and equity in policies and practices, and creating an environment where employees feel safe to speak up when they witness bias or discrimination.

Actively addressing bias and discrimination in the workplace is critical for creating a culture of inclusion and equity. It sends a clear message to employees that such behaviors will not be tolerated, and creates an environment where everyone feels valued, respected, and supported. Here are some reasons why it's important for leaders to actively address bias and discrimination:

Promotes a culture of inclusion: By addressing bias and discrimination, leaders can create a culture of inclusion where everyone feels welcome, respected, and valued. This can lead to higher employee engagement, retention, and productivity, and ultimately drive better business outcomes.

Mitigates the negative effects of bias and discrimination: Bias and discrimination can have a range of negative effects on employees, including reduced performance, disengagement, and attrition. By actively addressing these issues, leaders can help to mitigate these negative effects and promote a more positive and supportive workplace environment.

Builds Trust

Addressing bias and discrimination can help to build trust between leaders and employees. When employees see that their leaders are committed to promoting equity and inclusion, they are more likely to trust that their needs and concerns will be taken seriously.

Demonstrate your expressed commitment by addressing bias and discrimination in a tangible way. This can help to attract and retain employees from diverse backgrounds, who are more likely to seek out organizations that value and promote equity and inclusion.

Organizations that are known for their commitment to diversity and inclusion can enhance their reputation and appeal to customers, clients, and investors. By actively addressing bias and discrimination, leaders can help to enhance their organization's reputation as a diverse, equitable, and inclusive workplace.

Trust builds by actively addressing bias and discrimination is critical for promoting a culture of inclusion and equity in the workplace. By holding individuals accountable for discriminatory behavior, promoting fairness and equity in policies and practices, and creating an environment where employees feel safe to speak up, leaders can help to build trust, mitigate the negative effects of bias and discrimination, and demonstrate their commitment to diversity and inclusion.

Encourage Diverse Perspectives

Encouraging diverse perspectives and ideas can help to break down stereotypes and promote a more inclusive workplace culture. This includes creating opportunities for employees to share their experiences and ideas, and actively seeking out and valuing diverse perspectives in decision-making processes.

Encouraging diverse perspectives is crucial for promoting an inclusive workplace culture that values and leverages diversity. When individuals from different backgrounds and identities feel empowered to share their experiences and ideas, it can lead to more innovation, better problem-solving, and stronger relationships among colleagues.

Creating opportunities for employees to share their experiences and ideas is a key way to encourage diverse perspectives. This can involve creating forums for discussion, such as town halls, team meetings, or focus groups, where individuals can share their thoughts and ideas in a safe and supportive environment. Leaders can also encourage informal discussions and interactions among employees, such as through team-building activities, social events, or online collaboration tools.

Actively seeking out and valuing diverse perspectives is another important strategy for encouraging diverse perspectives. This involves actively soliciting input from employees, particularly those from underrepresented groups, and ensuring that diverse perspectives are represented in decision-making processes. This can help to break down stereotypes and biases and promote a more accurate and nuanced understanding of different groups.

To effectively encourage diverse perspectives, leaders should also be aware of their own biases and limitations. This involves being open to feedback and critique, and actively seeking out diverse perspectives and feedback on their own ideas and decisions. Leaders can also provide training and support to help employees develop the skills they need to engage in constructive and respectful dialogue, such as active listening, empathy, and communication skills.

By encouraging diverse perspectives, leaders can create a workplace culture where all employees feel valued, respected, and empowered to contribute their best work. This can lead to higher employee engagement, retention, and productivity, and ultimately drive better business outcomes.

Provide Growth and Development Opportunities

Providing growth and development opportunities can help employees to build confidence and improve their performance. This includes providing training and development opportunities, offering opportunities for career advancement, and providing regular feedback and coaching.

Providing growth and development opportunities is essential for retaining diverse employees and promoting their success in the workplace. By offering training and development opportunities, leaders can help employees to build their skills and knowledge, which can lead to increased confidence and improved performance.

One way to provide growth and development opportunities is through training and professional development programs. This can include courses, workshops, or online resources that are designed to help employees build new skills or enhance their existing ones. For example, providing training on leadership, communication, or project management can help employees to develop the skills they need to advance their careers and contribute to their organization.

Another way to provide growth and development opportunities is through offering opportunities for career advancement. This can involve providing clear career paths and opportunities for promotion, and actively supporting employees in achieving their career goals. This can help to promote employee engagement and retention, as employees are more likely to stay with an organization that values and invests in their career development.

Regular feedback and coaching is another important component of providing growth and development opportunities. This involves providing ongoing feedback and support to help employees identify their strengths and areas for improvement, and providing coaching or other forms of support to help them build their skills and improve their performance.

By providing growth and development opportunities, leaders can create a workplace culture that values and invests in its employees. This can lead to higher employee engagement, retention, and productivity, and ultimately drive better business outcomes. It is important for leaders to provide customized support that meets the unique needs and experiences of each employee, and to foster a culture of continuous learning and growth.

By adopting these strategies, leaders can create a workplace culture that values and leverages diversity, promotes equity and inclusion, and drives innovation and success. This can help to retain diverse employees and mitigate the impact of stereotype threat.

Key Strategies

Awareness

The first step in getting past stereotype threat is to be aware of its existence and the potential impact it can have on individuals' performance. This involves understanding the negative stereotypes that may be associated with different social identities and how they can create pressure or anxiety.

Affirmation

Affirmation involves acknowledging individuals' unique strengths and abilities, and promoting a sense of belonging and value in the workplace. This can be achieved through recognition of individuals' accomplishments, providing opportunities for growth and development, and creating an environment that is supportive and inclusive.

Counter-stereotyping

Counter-stereotyping involves challenging negative stereotypes and promoting more accurate and positive perceptions of different social identities. This can be achieved through education and awareness-raising, as well as through promoting diversity and inclusion in the workplace.

Self-regulation

Self-regulation involves developing strategies to manage the anxiety and pressure associated with stereotype threat. This can include techniques such as deep breathing, positive self-talk, and mindfulness practices.

Support

Support involves providing resources and support to individuals who may be experiencing stereotype threat. This can include coaching, mentorship, or other forms of support that help individuals to build confidence and improve their performance.

By using these strategies, individuals and organizations can work to get past stereotype threat and promote a more inclusive and equitable workplace culture. This can lead to higher employee engagement, retention, and productivity, and ultimately drive better business outcomes.

Stereotype threat and emotional intelligence are both important concepts that can impact an individual's performance in the workplace. Emotional intelligence involves the ability to recognize and manage one's own emotions, as well as the emotions of others. It is often viewed as a key factor in effective leadership and communication.

Research has shown that emotional intelligence can help individuals to better manage the pressure and anxiety associated with stereotype threat. By recognizing and managing their own emotions, individuals can better control the impact of negative stereotypes on their performance. Additionally, individuals with high emotional intelligence may be better able to recognize and respond to the emotions of others, which can help to create a more supportive and inclusive workplace environment.

Key Questions

What is stereotype threat?

Stereotype threat is a psychological phenomenon that occurs when individuals feel at risk of confirming a negative stereotype about their social group. This can lead to anxiety, reduced performance, and disengagement.

Who introduced the concept of stereotype threat?

The concept of stereotype threat was first introduced by social psychologists Claude Steele and Joshua Aronson in a 1995 paper titled "Stereotype Threat and the Intellectual Test Performance of African Americans".

What are stereotypes?

Stereotypes are social beliefs or expectations about certain groups of people, based on characteristics such as race, gender, age, or sexual orientation.

How can stereotype threat impact hiring?

Stereotype threat can influence both the hiring decisions of employers and the job-seeking behaviors of applicants. Employers may make biased hiring decisions based on negative stereotypes about certain groups of people, while individuals from stigmatized groups may be less likely to apply for jobs that are perceived as being dominated by another group.

What can employers do to mitigate the impact of stereotype threat on hiring?

Employers can adopt inclusive practices that promote diversity and equity, such as actively recruiting candidates from underrepresented groups, using inclusive language in job postings, and using diverse hiring panels to evaluate candidates. Employers can also provide training to help mitigate the effects of bias and stereotype threat on the hiring process.

How can leaders create a culture of inclusion to reduce the impact of stereotype threat?

Leaders can promote equity and diversity, provide opportunities for employees to connect and build relationships, and ensure that all employees feel valued and respected. By fostering a sense of belonging and value among all employees, leaders can help mitigate the negative effects of stereotype threat and promote a more diverse, equitable, and inclusive workplace.

What types of resources and support can be provided to employees to reduce the effects of stereotype threat?

Resources and support can include coaching, mentorship, training, professional development opportunities, and employee resource groups. These resources can help employees to build confidence, reduce anxiety, and improve their performance.

Why is it important for leaders to actively address bias and discrimination in the workplace?

Actively addressing bias and discrimination in the workplace promotes a culture of inclusion, mitigates the negative effects of bias and discrimination, and creates an environment where everyone feels valued, respected, and supported. This can lead to higher employee engagement, retention, and productivity, and ultimately drive better business outcomes.

Practice 6.1

Role Play Scenario:

Title
Overcoming Stereotype Threat in a Group Project

Setting
A college classroom where students are assigned to work in groups on a project. The groups are diverse, and some students may be experiencing stereotype threat based on their gender, race, or other social characteristics.

Characters
1. **Student A:** Feels anxious about the stereotype that their racial group is not good at math and might underperform in a statistics project.
2. **Student B:** Aware of the stereotype that women are not good leaders and is hesitant to take on a leadership role in the group.
3. **Student C:** A supportive and inclusive group member who wants to help mitigate stereotype threat for their peers.
4. **Student D:** Unaware of the concept of stereotype threat but is open to learning and becoming more inclusive.

Instructions
The role play will explore how the group members navigate the group project, addressing and overcoming stereotype threat, and creating an inclusive and supportive environment for all members. Each character should have an opportunity to express their thoughts, feelings, and ideas.

Role Play Outline

Group Introduction: The group members introduce themselves and start discussing the project. Student A and B may show signs of hesitation or anxiety.

Identifying Stereotype Threat: Student C notices the anxiety in Student A and B and gently brings up the topic of stereotype threat, explaining the concept to Student D and the rest of the group.

I AM: Stereotype Threat

Open Discussion: The group engages in an open discussion about their experiences with stereotypes and how they might impact their performance in the group project.

1. How did each group member's understanding of stereotype threat evolve throughout the role play, and how did it influence their interactions with one another?
2. What specific strategies did the group come up with to create an inclusive and supportive environment for all members?
3. How did Student A and Student B respond to the group's efforts to address stereotype threat? Did their performance and participation improve as a result?
4. How did Student C's leadership and understanding of stereotype threat contribute to the overall success of the group project?
5. Were there any moments during the group project when stereotype threat resurfaced, and how did the group address it?
6. In what ways did the open discussion about stereotype threat help the group members build trust and understanding among one another?
7. How did Student D's initial lack of knowledge about stereotype threat impact the group dynamic, and how did their perspective change as they learned more about the concept?
8. How did the group's experience with stereotype threat and their efforts to mitigate it affect the quality of their final project?
9. What lessons can be learned from this case study about the importance of addressing stereotype threat in diverse group settings?
10. How can educators and students apply the insights from this case study to create more inclusive and supportive learning environments in other contexts?

Practice 6.2

Group Activity

Building a Culture of Inclusion to Mitigate Stereotype Threat

Objective:

This learning activity aims to educate staff on the importance of creating a culture of inclusion, and equip them with the tools and strategies needed to reduce the impact of stereotype threat in the workplace.

Duration

2 hours

Materials

- Whiteboard or flipchart
- Markers
- Sticky notes
- Handout on stereotype threat and inclusion (based on the provided text)
- Projector or screen for videos (optional)

Activity Outline

1. Introduction (10 minutes)
   - Begin with a brief introduction to stereotype threat and its impact on employees.
   - Discuss the importance of creating a culture of inclusion to mitigate stereotype threat.
   - Provide an overview of the learning activity and its objectives.

2. Understanding Stereotype Threat (20 minutes)
   - Divide participants into small groups.
   - Distribute the handout on stereotype threat and inclusion.
   - Ask participants to read the handout and discuss their understanding of stereotype threat, its consequences, and the importance of inclusion.
   - Reconvene and ask each group to share their insights with the larger group.

3. Promoting Equity and Diversity (30 minutes)
   - Lead a discussion on policies and practices that promote equity and diversity in the workplace, such as pay equity, diverse hiring and promotion practices, and anti-discrimination policies.
   - Encourage participants to brainstorm other ways to promote equity and diversity within their organization.
   - Optional: Show a short video on the benefits of promoting equity and diversity in the workplace.

4. Fostering Connection and Building Relationships (30 minutes)
   - Ask participants to brainstorm team-building activities, social events, and other opportunities to help employees connect and build relationships.
   - Encourage participants to consider activities that are inclusive of diverse backgrounds and interests.
   - Divide participants into pairs or small groups to share their ideas and discuss their potential impact on the workplace.

5. Ensuring Employees Feel Valued and Respected (20 minutes)
   - Lead a discussion on the importance of treating all employees with respect and dignity.
   - Ask participants to brainstorm ways to recognize and celebrate the contributions of all employees, creating a workplace culture where everyone's contributions are valued and recognized.
   - Optional: Show a short video on the impact of feeling valued and respected in the workplace.

6. Action Plan (10 minutes)
   - Ask participants to reflect on what they've learned and create a personal action plan to promote a culture of inclusion within their organization.
   - Encourage participants to write down three specific actions they will take to promote equity and diversity, foster connection and relationships, and ensure all employees feel valued and respected.
   - Have participants share their action plans with a partner or small group for feedback and accountability.

7. Closing (10 minutes)
   - Reconvene the large group and ask for volunteers to share their action plans.
   - Summarize the key takeaways from the learning activity.
   - Encourage participants to put their action plans into practice and continue the conversation with their colleagues and leaders.

Practice 6.3

Group Activity
Overcoming Stereotype Threat: Strategies for New Leaders

Objective:
This activity aims to help new leaders understand the concept of stereotype threat and develop strategies to overcome it, promote inclusion, and enhance emotional intelligence in the workplace.

Duration
2 hours

Materials
- Flipchart or whiteboard
- Markers
- Sticky notes
- Handout on stereotype threat, strategies, and emotional intelligence (based on the provided text)

Activity Outline

1. Introduction (10 minutes)
   - Begin with a brief introduction to stereotype threat and its potential impact on individuals' performance.
   - Discuss the importance of overcoming stereotype threat and promoting inclusion in the workplace.
   - Provide an overview of the learning activity and its objectives.

2. Understanding Stereotype Threat (20 minutes)
   - Divide participants into small groups.
   - Distribute the handout on stereotype threat, strategies, and emotional intelligence.
   - Ask participants to read the handout and discuss their understanding of stereotype threat and its consequences.
   - Reconvene and ask each group to share their insights with the larger group.

3. Developing Strategies to Overcome Stereotype Threat (60 minutes)
   - Introduce the five strategies for overcoming stereotype threat: Awareness, Affirmation, Counter-stereotyping, Self-regulation, and Support.
   - Divide participants into five groups, assigning each group one of the strategies.
   - Ask each group to brainstorm and discuss ways to implement their assigned strategy in the workplace.
   - Reconvene and have each group present their findings to the larger group.
   - Facilitate a discussion on how these strategies can be applied collectively to create a more inclusive work environment.

4. Emotional Intelligence and Stereotype Threat (20 minutes)
   - Lead a discussion on the role of emotional intelligence in managing stereotype threat and promoting a supportive work environment.
   - Ask participants to share their thoughts on how they can develop their emotional intelligence to better respond to the emotions of others and create an inclusive workplace.
   - Optional: Show a short video on the importance of emotional intelligence in the workplace.

5. Action Plan (10 minutes)
   - Ask participants to reflect on what they've learned and create a personal action plan for implementing the strategies to overcome stereotype threat and enhance their emotional intelligence.
   - Encourage participants to write down three specific actions they will take in their leadership role.
   - Have participants share their action plans with a partner or small group for feedback and accountability.

6. Closing (10 minutes)
   - Reconvene the large group and ask for volunteers to share their action plans.
   - Summarize the key takeaways from the learning activity.
   - Encourage participants to put their action plans into practice and continue the conversation with their colleagues and leaders.

Answer Key 6.1

1. Throughout the role play, each group member's understanding of stereotype threat evolved as they discussed their experiences and shared their concerns. Their interactions with one another became more empathetic and supportive as they recognized the impact of stereotype threat on their peers.

2. The group came up with several strategies to create an inclusive and supportive environment, such as emphasizing collaboration, assigning tasks based on individual strengths, fostering open communication, and encouraging all members to contribute their ideas and perspectives.

3. Student A and Student B responded positively to the group's efforts to address stereotype threat. They felt more comfortable participating in the project, and their performance improved as their anxiety diminished.

4. Student C's leadership and understanding of stereotype threat played a crucial role in the group's success. They facilitated open discussions, encouraged collaboration, and helped to create an inclusive environment that allowed all group members to thrive.

5. There may have been moments when stereotype threat resurfaced during the project, but the group was able to address it by maintaining open communication, reiterating their commitment to inclusivity, and offering support to one another.

6. The open discussion about stereotype threat helped build trust and understanding among group members by allowing them to share their experiences, acknowledge their vulnerabilities, and find common ground in their desire to create a positive group dynamic.

7. Student D's initial lack of knowledge about stereotype threat may have initially contributed to some misunderstandings or unintentional reinforcement of stereotypes. However, as they learned more about the concept and listened to their peers, their perspective changed, and they became more sensitive to the experiences of others.

8. The group's experience with stereotype threat and their efforts to mitigate it positively affected the quality of their final project. By creating an inclusive and supportive environment, they were able to collaborate more effectively, draw on the unique strengths of each member, and produce a high-quality project.

9. The case study highlights the importance of addressing stereotype threat in diverse group settings, as it can impact performance and participation. By fostering open communication and creating an inclusive environment, groups can mitigate stereotype threat and enhance the success of their projects.

10. Educators and students can apply the insights from this case study by promoting awareness of stereotype threat, encouraging open discussions about stereotypes and their effects, and implementing inclusive practices in their classrooms and group projects. This can help create more inclusive and supportive learning environments that benefit all students.

"Throughlines"

Dear Boss,

I hope this message finds you well. I am writing to bring to your attention an issue that I believe is crucial to the success and wellbeing of our organization: the impact of racism and the ecosystem it thrives in through current workplace behavior.

In recent times, our society has become increasingly aware of the prevalence and detrimental effects of racism, and it has become more important than ever for organizations to actively tackle this issue. As a part of our school's commitment to diversity and inclusion, I would like to share an experience with you.

I recently joined the marketing team in weekly meetings, noting that most employees are white, while I am Black and Latino. During one of those team meetings, I had the opportunity to deliver a presentation on a new marketing strategy. After my presentation, one of my colleagues, Anna, approached me and complimented my work. She said, "Christopher, you are so articulate! I didn't expect your presentation to be so clear and well-structured."

While I appreciated her positive feedback, I couldn't help but feel that her surprise at my communication skills implied an *underlying assumption about people of Black/Latino descent. It was as if she didn't expect someone like me to be capable of delivering a professional and well-organized presentation. This experience highlighted the subtle ways that microaggressions can manifest in the workplace, making me feel singled out and invalidated despite the seemingly well-intentioned nature of the comment.*

Microaggressions are subtle, often unintentional, discriminatory behaviors that can make individuals from marginalized groups feel invalidated or unwelcome. It is essential for us to first name the aggression and then provide training and resources to help colleagues recognize and address these microaggressions in order to create a more inclusive environment.

Thank you for reading,

Christopher

Chapter 7
Ecosystem of Racism

Systemic racism refers to a pattern of racism that is built into the systems and structures of society, including laws, policies, and practices, that result in unequal outcomes for different racial groups. Unlike individual acts of racism, which are typically committed by individuals, systemic racism operates at a broader level and can be more difficult to identify and address.

Systemic racism can manifest in many ways, including disparities in access to quality employment opportunities and experiences. It can also lead to overrepresentation of certain racial groups in non leadership roles.

One key aspect of systemic racism is that it is often perpetuated unconsciously by individuals who may not be aware of the impact of their actions on different racial groups. This is why it is important to acknowledge and address systemic racism, as well as to actively work towards creating more equitable systems and structures that promote equal outcomes for all individuals, regardless of their race.

The ecological framework provides a framework for understanding how systemic racism can impact individuals and communities at work. According to the ecological framework, individuals exist within multiple interconnected systems, including the microsystem (individual interactions and relationships), mesosystem (interactions between different systems), exosystem (external systems that impact individuals indirectly), and macrosystem (larger cultural and societal systems).

The ecosystem of racism is a term used to describe how systemic racism operates at all levels of the ecological framework. It affects individuals, institutions, organizations, societal factors, and cultural beliefs and attitudes about race and ethnicity. At the microsystem level, individuals may experience discrimination and prejudice based on their race or ethnicity. At the mesosystem level, institutions and organizations may perpetuate systemic racism through policies and practices that disproportionately disadvantage certain racial or ethnic groups. At the exosystem level, societal factors such as housing discrimination or unequal access to education can limit opportunities for certain groups of individuals. Finally, at the macrosystem level, cultural beliefs and attitudes about race and ethnicity can perpetuate systemic racism through social norms and values. Understanding the ecosystem of racism and how it operates at various levels is crucial in addressing systemic racism and promoting equity and inclusion for all individuals.

Microsystem

The microsystem refers to the immediate environment in which individuals live and work. In the workplace, this includes the physical space, the people they interact with (such as coworkers and managers), and the tasks they perform. The quality of these factors can have a significant impact on an employee's experience at work.

The microsystem component of the ecological framework can help explain the impact of the immediate work environment on the retention of diverse candidates. One significant factor is the lack of diversity in the workplace. When a workplace lacks diversity, diverse candidates may struggle to find a sense of belonging and connection with their coworkers, leading to feelings of isolation and disengagement. This can ultimately lead to a decision to leave the job.

Discrimination and bias can also impact diverse candidates' retention. Diverse candidates may experience discrimination or bias from their coworkers or managers, which can make them feel unwelcome and undervalued. This can lead to a lack of motivation and engagement, ultimately impacting retention. Negative comments or jokes about an employee's sexual orientation, for example, can lead to a decrease in motivation and engagement over time.

Limited career advancement opportunities can also be a significant factor in diverse candidates' retention. When diverse candidates feel that they have limited opportunities for career advancement, they may feel like their potential is not being fully utilized, leading to a lack of motivation and engagement. This can ultimately lead to the employee leaving the company for a workplace that offers more opportunities for growth and career advancement.

Poor management practices can also contribute to a negative work environment, impacting the retention of all employees, including diverse candidates. When managers do not provide clear expectations, support, or recognition to their employees, they may feel undervalued and unappreciated, impacting their decision to stay with the company. A lack of communication and recognition from a manager can lead to a negative work environment that impacts employee morale and motivation.

Employers should consider addressing these microsystem factors to create a more welcoming, inclusive, and supportive workplace that values and supports diversity. This may include promoting diversity and inclusion training, addressing discrimination and bias, providing opportunities for career advancement, and improving management practices. By addressing these factors, employers can create a positive work environment that supports and builds a resilient and inclusive workplace.

Mesosystem

The mesosystem refers to the relationships between different parts of an individual's microsystem. In the workplace, this includes the relationships between employees and their coworkers, as well as between employees and their managers. The quality of these relationships can impact an employee's job satisfaction and overall well-being.

The mesosystem component of the ecological framework can help explain why diverse candidates may have low retention rates in a workplace. Relationships between different parts of an individual's microsystem, including coworkers and managers, are crucial to the mesosystem's functioning. Negative interpersonal relationships, limited social support, lack of mentorship, and poor communication practices are some of the ways the mesosystem can impact the retention of diverse candidates.

Negative interpersonal relationships can impact diverse candidates' retention. Bullying, harassment, or exclusion can lead to a lack of trust, support, and engagement, ultimately impacting their decision to stay with the company. These negative interactions can make diverse candidates feel unsupported, unwelcome, and isolated in the workplace, leading to disengagement and a lack of motivation.

Limited social support can also contribute to diverse candidates' retention issues. When diverse candidates belong to a demographic group that is not well represented in the company, they may struggle to establish connections and relationships with their coworkers, leading to a lack of belonging and engagement. This limited social support can impact their decision to stay with the company and seek out a more supportive and inclusive work environment.

Lack of mentorship can impact diverse candidates' retention rates by limiting their ability to learn new skills, grow professionally, and develop relationships with others in the workplace. Without access to mentorship opportunities, diverse candidates may feel like they are not being given the opportunities they need to succeed and grow within the company, leading to a lack of satisfaction and commitment to their job.

Poor communication practices can also impact the retention of diverse candidates. When there are poor communication practices, such as unclear expectations or inconsistent feedback, it can lead to misunderstandings and conflicts between employees and their managers or coworkers. This can compound diverse candidates' negative experiences and lead to disengagement and a lack of motivation.

Employers should consider addressing these mesosystem factors to create a more supportive and inclusive workplace that values and supports diversity. This may include promoting positive interpersonal relationships, providing mentorship opportunities, improving communication practices, and creating opportunities for social support. By addressing these factors, employers can create a positive work environment that supports the retention of diverse candidates and contributes to a more diverse and inclusive workplace.

Exosystem

The exosystem refers to the broader social, economic, and cultural factors that impact an individual's microsystem. In the workplace, this includes things like government policies, economic conditions, and cultural attitudes towards work. These factors can impact an employee's job security, compensation, and overall sense of belonging within the workplace.

The exosystem component of the ecological framework plays an important role in understanding why diverse candidates may have low retention rates in a workplace. The exosystem encompasses the broader social, economic, and cultural factors that impact an individual's microsystem, including government policies, economic conditions, and cultural attitudes towards work.

Discrimination in society is one of the key factors that can impact diverse candidates' sense of worth and value. When diverse candidates experience discrimination and prejudice in society based on their identity, they may bring these negative experiences and feelings into the workplace. Over time, this can impact their sense of worth and value in the workplace, leading to a lack of engagement and motivation in their job, and may ultimately impact their decision to stay with the company.

Limited access to education and training is another factor that can impact the retention of diverse candidates. Diverse candidates may have limited access to education and training opportunities that can help them improve their skills and knowledge. This can impact their ability to compete for and succeed in high-paying, rewarding jobs within the company, which can lead to a lack of satisfaction and commitment to their job.

The lack of government policies and support for diversity and inclusion initiatives is another key factor that can impact the retention of diverse candidates in the workplace. If there are no policies in place to support diversity and inclusion, the workplace may not prioritize these efforts, leading to a lack of resources and support for diverse candidates. Over time, this can impact the employee's motivation and engagement in the workplace, leading to a lack of satisfaction and commitment to their job.

Economic conditions can also impact the retention of diverse candidates. When job security is low, diverse candidates may be more likely to leave the company for a more stable job opportunity. Economic conditions such as recessions, layoffs, and hiring freezes can impact the job security of all employees, including diverse candidates. Over time, this can impact the employee's motivation and engagement in the workplace, leading to a lack of satisfaction and commitment to their job.

In order to address these exosystem factors, employers should consider implementing policies and programs to support diversity and inclusion initiatives, providing education and training opportunities to diverse candidates, and creating a more stable work environment. By creating a more supportive and inclusive workplace that values and supports diversity, employers can help retain diverse candidates and contribute to a more diverse and successful workplace.

Macrosystem

The macrosystem refers to the larger cultural and societal context in which an individual exists. In the workplace, this includes broader cultural attitudes towards work and the economy, as well as the impact of global events on the workplace. These factors can impact an employee's sense of purpose and motivation in their work.

The ecological framework suggests that a wide range of factors can impact an employee's experience at work, from the physical environment to broader cultural attitudes towards work. Employers can use this framework to better understand and address the needs of their employees, creating a more positive and productive work environment.

The macrosystem component of the ecological framework can help explain why diverse candidates may have low retention rates in a workplace. The macrosystem refers to the cultural, social, and political ideologies and values that shape the broader society. In the context of the workplace, this includes things like cultural norms around work, societal attitudes towards diversity and inclusion, and political ideologies that shape employment policies.

One way the macrosystem can impact the retention of diverse candidates is through systemic racism and discrimination. Diverse candidates may experience these negative factors in society, which can make it difficult to succeed in the workplace. Over time, this can impact their sense of worth and value, lead to a lack of engagement and motivation in their job, and ultimately impact their decision to stay with the company. Addressing systemic racism and discrimination in society and in the workplace is crucial for creating an inclusive and supportive work environment for all employees.

Limited representation in leadership positions is another way the macrosystem can impact the retention of diverse candidates. A lack of diverse representation can make it difficult for diverse employees to see themselves in leadership roles and feel like they have opportunities for career advancement within the company. Over time, this limited representation can impact the employee's sense of belonging and engagement in the workplace, which can lead to a lack of motivation and commitment to their job. Promoting diversity and inclusion in leadership positions can help create a more inclusive and supportive work environment for all employees.

Political ideologies and policies can also impact the retention of diverse candidates. If there are no policies in place to support diversity and inclusion initiatives, the workplace may not prioritize these efforts. This can make it difficult for diverse candidates to feel valued and supported, and impact their motivation and engagement in the workplace. Employers should take the time to understand and address the impact of political ideologies and policies on their workplace culture, and work to create policies and initiatives that support diversity and inclusion for all employees.

Cultural norms around work, such as long work hours, a focus on individual achievement, and a lack of work-life balance, can also impact the retention of diverse candidates who may have different cultural values and priorities. This can create a work environment that is challenging for diverse candidates who may value time with family or a more collaborative work environment. Over time, these cultural norms can impact the employee's motivation and engagement in the workplace, and ultimately impact their decision to stay with the company. Creating a work environment that is inclusive and supportive of diverse cultural values and priorities can help support the retention of all employees.

In conclusion, the macrosystem component of the ecological framework can help employers understand the broader societal factors that impact the retention of diverse candidates. Employers should consider addressing these macrosystem factors, such as promoting diverse representation in leadership positions, supporting political policies that prioritize diversity and inclusion initiatives, and creating a more flexible work environment that accommodates different cultural norms and priorities. This will help create a more supportive and inclusive workplace that values and supports diversity for all employees.

Application

Applying an ecological framework can help organizations enhance the conditions for employees by considering the multiple factors that impact their well-being and productivity, which includes their physical surroundings, social relationships, organizational policies and practices, as well as the broader cultural and societal factors.

Physical environment

Ensure that the workplace is safe and conducive to productivity. This can include providing adequate lighting, ventilation, and ergonomic furniture. Additionally, providing access to healthy food options and opportunities for physical activity can support employee well-being.

Social Relationships

Encourage positive social relationships among employees by fostering a culture of respect, inclusivity, and collaboration. This can be achieved through team-building activities, regular feedback, and open communication channels.

Organizational Policies and Practices

Implement policies and practices that prioritize employee well-being, such as flexible work arrangements, opportunities for career development, and fair compensation and benefits packages. Providing training and development opportunities can also help employees build skills and feel valued.

Broader Cultural and Societal Factors

Address systemic issues that may impact employee well-being, such as discrimination, harassment, and inequality. This can involve creating policies that promote diversity, equity, and inclusion, as well as advocating for broader societal changes that support worker rights and social justice.

By considering these various factors and taking a holistic approach, organizations can create a more supportive and sustainable work environment that benefits both employees and the broader community.

THROUGHLINES: ECOSYSTEM OF RACISM

Key Questions

What is the main difference between systemic racism and individual acts of racism?

The main difference between systemic racism and individual acts of racism is that systemic racism is built into the systems and structures of society, operating at a broader level, while individual acts of racism are typically committed by individuals.

How does systemic racism manifest in the workplace?

Systemic racism in the workplace can manifest in various ways, including disparities in access to quality employment opportunities and experiences, overrepresentation of certain racial groups in non-leadership roles, discrimination, and bias.

How does the ecological framework help in understanding the impact of systemic racism on individuals and communities at work?

The ecological framework helps by illustrating that individuals exist within multiple interconnected systems, such as the microsystem, mesosystem, exosystem, and macrosystem. These systems interact to create the ecosystem of racism, which can impact individuals at various levels, from individual interactions to larger cultural and societal systems.

What are some factors that can impact the retention of diverse candidates at the microsystem level?

Factors impacting the retention of diverse candidates at the microsystem level include a lack of diversity in the workplace, discrimination and bias, limited career advancement opportunities, and poor management practices.

What actions can employers take to address microsystem factors and create a more inclusive and supportive workplace?

Employers can promote diversity and inclusion training, address discrimination and bias, provide opportunities for career advancement, and improve management practices to create a more inclusive and supportive workplace.

What is the role of the mesosystem in the workplace, and how does it affect employees?

The mesosystem refers to the relationships between different parts of an individual's microsystem, such as the relationships between employees and their coworkers, as well as between employees and their managers. The quality of these relationships can impact an employee's job satisfaction and overall well-being.

How can unconscious actions by individuals perpetuate systemic racism?

Unconscious actions can perpetuate systemic racism because individuals may not be aware of the impact of their actions on different racial groups. This lack of awareness can lead to the continuation of biased behaviors, policies, and practices that contribute to unequal outcomes for different racial groups.

How does the ecosystem of racism operate at the exosystem level?

At the exosystem level, societal factors such as housing discrimination or unequal access to education can limit opportunities for certain groups of individuals, contributing to systemic racism.

What role do cultural beliefs and attitudes play in perpetuating systemic racism at the macrosystem level?

At the macrosystem level, cultural beliefs and attitudes about race and ethnicity can perpetuate systemic racism through social norms and values. These norms and values may shape the way individuals perceive and interact with different racial and ethnic groups, reinforcing stereotypes and biases.

What are some specific strategies employers can use to improve the mesosystem in the workplace?

Employers can improve the mesosystem in the workplace by fostering open communication, encouraging teamwork, promoting mentorship programs, providing conflict resolution training, and creating opportunities for employees to build relationships with coworkers and managers from diverse backgrounds.

Practice 7.1

Samantha is a Black woman who has been working at a large corporation for several years. Despite her hard work and dedication to her job, she has noticed that her opportunities for advancement are limited. Most of the leadership positions are held by white individuals, and there are few people of color in higher-level roles.

Samantha has also noticed that there are disparities in the treatment of employees of different races. Black employees often have more menial tasks and are given less challenging assignments, while white employees are given more opportunities for growth and development.

These experiences have made Samantha feel undervalued and unsupported in her workplace. She has also experienced instances of microaggressions and discrimination from her coworkers, such as being asked to speak for all Black people during meetings or being told that she is "articulate" for a Black person.

Upon further investigation, Samantha learns that the company's policies and practices are not inclusive of diverse perspectives and that there are few efforts to address systemic racism within the organization. Many of the policies and practices are based on assumptions about what works for white employees and do not take into account the unique experiences and needs of employees of color.

Samantha decides to speak up and advocate for change within the company. She connects with other employees of color and forms an employee resource group focused on promoting diversity and inclusion. They gather data on the experiences of diverse employees and present their findings to upper management, along with recommendations for more equitable policies and practices.

While the road to change is not easy, Samantha and her colleagues are able to make some progress. The company starts implementing diversity and inclusion training for all employees and begins to re-evaluate some of its policies and practices to ensure they are inclusive of all perspectives. Samantha is also able to connect with other Black women in leadership positions within the company, who serve as mentors and advocates for her career growth.

Through Samantha's experiences, it becomes clear how systemic racism operates at various levels of the ecological framework. The company's policies and practices perpetuate systemic racism through their effects on individuals and institutions, while societal factors like housing discrimination and unequal access to education also impact opportunities for individuals of color. Ultimately, by acknowledging and addressing systemic racism and promoting more equitable policies and practices, organizations can create a more inclusive and supportive work environment for all employees.

1. How has Samantha been impacted by systemic racism in her workplace?
2. What disparities has Samantha observed in the treatment of employees of different races?
3. How has Samantha advocated for change within her organization?
4. What progress has Samantha and her colleagues been able to make in addressing systemic racism within their organization?
5. How has the company responded to the recommendations made by Samantha and her colleagues?
6. How does the ecological framework help us understand the impact of systemic racism in the workplace?
7. What are some of the societal factors that can impact opportunities for individuals of color in the workplace?
8. What are some ways that organizations can promote more equitable policies and practices to create a more inclusive and supportive work environment?

Practice 7.2

Group Activity
Analyzing the Impact of the Macrosystem on Employee Retention

Objective:
This activity aims to help participants understand the impact of macrosystem factors on the retention of diverse candidates and develop strategies to create a more inclusive and supportive work environment.

Materials
- Flipchart
- Markers
- Sticky notes
- Pens

Activity Outline

1. Divide participants into small groups of 4-5 people.

2. Assign each group one of the following macrosystem factors:
   - Systemic racism and discrimination
   - Limited representation in leadership positions
   - Political ideologies and policies
   - Cultural norms around work

3. Ask each group to brainstorm and discuss the impact of their assigned factor on the retention of diverse candidates within a workplace. Encourage groups to consider both the negative and positive aspects of their factor and how it influences employee motivation, engagement, and commitment.

4. Next, instruct each group to come up with strategies to address the challenges posed by their assigned factor and create a more inclusive and supportive work environment for all employees.

5. Have each group present their findings and strategies to the larger group. Encourage a discussion about the commonalities and differences between the groups' findings and explore how organizations can implement these strategies in practice.

6. As a final step, provide each participant with a sticky note and pen. Ask them to write down one actionable step they can personally take to promote diversity and inclusion within their workplace, considering the macrosystem factors discussed in the activity.

7. Collect the sticky notes and post them on a designated wall or board, creating a visual representation of the group's commitment to fostering an inclusive and supportive work environment.

By engaging in this activity, participants will gain a better understanding of the impact of macrosystem factors on employee retention and develop strategies to create a more inclusive and supportive work environment that values and supports diversity for all employees.

Throughlines: Ecosystem of Racism

Answer Key 7.1

1. Samantha has been impacted by systemic racism in her workplace in multiple ways. She has noticed that her opportunities for advancement are limited, and most leadership positions are held by white individuals. Additionally, she has observed disparities in the treatment of employees of different races, with Black employees often having more menial tasks and being given less challenging assignments. Samantha has also experienced instances of microaggressions and discrimination from her coworkers, which have made her feel undervalued and unsupported.

2. Samantha has observed that Black employees often have more menial tasks and are given less challenging assignments than their white counterparts. She has also noticed that there are disparities in the treatment of employees of different races, with white employees being given more opportunities for growth and development.

3. Samantha has advocated for change within her organization by connecting with other employees of color and forming an employee resource group focused on promoting diversity and inclusion. They gathered data on the experiences of diverse employees and presented their findings to upper management, along with recommendations for more equitable policies and practices.

4. Samantha and her colleagues have been able to make some progress in addressing systemic racism within their organization. The company started implementing diversity and inclusion training for all employees and began to re-evaluate some of its policies and practices to ensure they are inclusive of all perspectives.

5. The company responded to the recommendations made by Samantha and her colleagues by implementing diversity and inclusion training for all employees and beginning to re-evaluate some of its policies and practices to ensure they are inclusive of all perspectives.

6. The ecological framework helps us understand the impact of systemic racism in the workplace by showing how systemic racism operates at various levels, including the microsystem, mesosystem, exosystem, and macrosystem. It affects individuals, institutions, organizations, societal factors, and cultural beliefs and attitudes about race and ethnicity.

7. Some of the societal factors that can impact opportunities for individuals of color in the workplace include housing discrimination, unequal access to education, and systemic racism within the criminal justice system.

8. Organizations can promote more equitable policies and practices by implementing diversity and inclusion training for all employees, re-evaluating policies and practices to ensure they are inclusive of all perspectives, and creating employee resource groups focused on promoting diversity and inclusion. They can also gather data on the experiences of diverse employees and use it to inform their decision-making.

"Investments"

ILO Institute developed a comprehensive DEI strategy that included training, mentoring, and feedback initiatives to support employees of color and create a more inclusive workplace.

As part of the feedback initiative, the institution implemented a 360-degree feedback system that allowed employees to receive feedback from multiple sources, including colleagues, managers, and clients. The feedback was designed to be objective, specific, and actionable, focusing on areas such as communication, teamwork, and leadership.

Employees of color were encouraged to participate in the feedback system, and the institution provided additional support and resources to help them interpret and use the feedback effectively. The institution also implemented a coaching program to help employees of color develop strategies to address any issues identified in the feedback.

One specific example of the impact of the feedback system was with a Black employee who was struggling with communication and collaboration with colleagues. After receiving feedback from multiple sources, including colleagues and clients, the employee participated in a coaching session to develop a plan for improvement.

The coaching session focused on specific strategies for improving communication and building stronger relationships with colleagues. The employee was also provided with additional training on effective communication and conflict resolution.

Over time, the employee's performance and engagement improved significantly. They were able to build stronger relationships with colleagues, communicate more effectively, and contribute to the success of the team. The employee also felt more supported and valued by the institution, leading to increased job satisfaction and commitment.

Overall, the feedback system was a powerful tool for supporting employees of color and creating a more inclusive workplace. It allowed for objective, specific, and actionable feedback, which was supported by coaching and training to help employees improve their performance and develop strategies for success.

Chapter 8
Cybernetics

The concept of feedback has been around for centuries, and its origins can be traced back to various fields and disciplines. The term "cybernetics" was coined by the mathematician and philosopher Norbert Wiener in 1948. He derived the term from the Greek word "kubernētēs" (κυβερνήτης), which means "steersman" or "governor." Wiener introduced the term in his groundbreaking book "Cybernetics: or Control and Communication in the Animal and the Machine."

Cybernetics is a transdisciplinary approach to studying and understanding the principles of communication, control, and feedback in living organisms, machines, and social systems. It examines the way systems regulate themselves through self-corrective feedback loops, and how information is processed and transmitted within and between systems.

In the engineering field, cybernetics can be traced back to the development of automatic control systems in the late 19th century. Engineers realized that in order to control complex systems, they needed a way to monitor and adjust their performance in real-time. They developed feedback loops, which allowed them to sense changes in the system and make adjustments to ensure optimal performance.

In the field of psychology, cybernetics became popular in the mid-20th century as a way to improve performance and behavior. Psychologists and educators began using feedback as a tool to help individuals understand their strengths and weaknesses, set goals, and track progress towards those goals.

Today, cybernetics, or feedback, is a widely used tool in a variety of fields, including business, education, sports, and personal development. Its origins in engineering and psychology have influenced the ways in which it is used, with a focus on monitoring and adjusting performance, and providing guidance and support for improvement. Feedback has become an essential tool for personal and professional growth, and its importance is widely recognized across a variety of fields.

Feedback is a term used to describe information or comments about the performance of a person or an organization, provided to them by others who have interacted with or observed their performance. It is a way to offer constructive criticism or praise to help individuals or organizations improve their performance, behaviors, or results. Feedback can be given in a variety of forms, including verbal, written, or through nonverbal cues, and can be both positive and negative. Feedback is often used in workplace settings to promote learning, growth, and development, and it can be a powerful tool for improving performance and achieving goals.

Feedback refers to the information or response given to someone about their actions, behavior, or performance. It is a communication process in which an individual or group receives information about their behavior or performance and uses that information to make adjustments and improve. Feedback can be positive, negative, or neutral, and can be delivered in various forms, such as verbal or written comments, ratings, evaluations, or assessments. The purpose of feedback is to facilitate learning, growth, and development by providing insight into areas where improvement is needed or where strengths can be built upon.

Many of the strategies presented play a significant role in building a resilient workforce. All of the approaches can be further enhanced by incorporating employee feedback, which research suggests is an essential component of a successful and productive workplace.

Employee feedback contributes to increased performance, as studies have found that employees who receive regular feedback tend to perform better and are more engaged in their work. Feedback helps employees understand what they are doing well and where they need to improve, which can motivate them to work harder and achieve better results. By implementing intersectional leadership and equity-based hiring, organizations can ensure that feedback is provided to employees from diverse backgrounds, promoting equal opportunities for growth and development.

In addition to improving performance, feedback also promotes better communication between employees and their managers or colleagues. This improved communication can be especially beneficial in diverse workplaces, where understanding different perspectives and addressing concerns is crucial to building trust and improving relationships. Employees who feel heard and understood are more likely to stay with their current employer, resulting in higher retention rates.

Feedback is also an important tool for learning and development by providing feedback to employees from diverse backgrounds, organizations can support their professional growth and help them identify areas where they need to improve. This can lead to increased skill development and career advancement, ultimately contributing to a more diverse and inclusive workplace.

Feedback can promote innovation and creativity in the workplace. Encouraging employees to think outside the box and share their ideas can lead to new and innovative solutions. In the context of intersectional leadership and equity-based hiring, this can help organizations tap into the unique perspectives and experiences of a diverse workforce, fostering an environment of innovation and growth.

The combination of theories and frameworks with a strong emphasis on employee feedback can create a more inclusive and successful workplace. These strategies promote better performance, communication, retention, learning, and innovation, ultimately contributing to a diverse and thriving organizational culture.

TARGETED FEEDBACK

Feedback is crucial for leaders of color in today's diverse workplace. By understanding and embracing the value of feedback, leaders can address biases and foster a more inclusive work environment. One essential aspect of feedback for leaders of color is its role in addressing both implicit and explicit biases. By identifying areas where bias may be affecting perceptions, leaders can work to rectify these issues and ensure fair evaluations. This increased awareness can also help leaders navigate potential challenges and excel in their roles.

Another important benefit of feedback for leaders of color is the opportunity to build trust with colleagues. By demonstrating openness to criticism and a willingness to learn and improve, these leaders can foster strong relationships within their teams. This trust is vital for creating a positive and supportive work environment where everyone feels valued.

Feedback can also help leaders of color identify blind spots they may not be aware of, such as unconscious biases or areas where their effectiveness could be improved. By addressing these blind spots, leaders can become more self-aware and refine their approach, ultimately contributing to their success and the success of their teams.

Developing skills is another area where feedback can be invaluable for leaders of color. Through constructive feedback, they can identify areas that need improvement and receive guidance on how to enhance their performance. This continuous learning process can lead to professional growth and better decision-making.

Lastly, feedback plays a critical role in creating a supportive environment for leaders of color. By fostering open communication and encouraging the sharing of experiences, ideas, and concerns, leaders can cultivate a collaborative atmosphere where diverse perspectives are valued. This inclusive environment can lead to more effective decision-making and improved overall team performance.

Feedback is a powerful tool for leaders of color, enabling them to address biases, build trust, identify blind spots, develop skills, and create a supportive work environment. By embracing feedback and fostering a culture of learning, these leaders can contribute to the success of their teams and organizations while promoting inclusivity and diversity.

VALUE ADDED

To maximize the effectiveness of feedback in improving learning, it is important to ensure that feedback is timely, specific, and actionable.

Feedback should be focused on behaviors or actions that can be changed, rather than on personal traits or characteristics. Additionally, feedback should be delivered in a supportive and constructive manner, with an emphasis on learning and development. By incorporating feedback into the learning process, individuals and organizations can improve their performance and achieve their goals.

Research has shown that employees who receive regular feedback and recognition are more likely to feel valued and engaged in their work, which can lead to greater job satisfaction and commitment to the organization.

When employees receive feedback, they gain a better understanding of their strengths and weaknesses and the areas where they need to improve. This can help them develop their skills and grow professionally, which can increase their job satisfaction and motivation to stay with the organization.

Additionally, feedback can help employees feel more connected to their colleagues and managers. When employees receive feedback that is constructive and supportive, it can help them feel that they are part of a team that cares about their success. This sense of connection can lead to increased loyalty and commitment to the organization.

On the other hand, when employees do not receive feedback or feel that their contributions are not recognized or valued, they may become disengaged and less committed to the organization. This can lead to increased turnover and reduced productivity, which can be costly for the organization.

Overall, feedback can be a powerful tool for improving employee retention by helping employees feel valued, supported, and connected to the organization. By providing regular feedback, organizations can improve employee engagement, job satisfaction, and commitment, leading to greater productivity and success.

One scenario of ineffective feedback is when a manager provides vague or general feedback to an employee, without specific examples or suggestions for improvement.

For example, a manager may tell an employee, "You need to improve your communication skills," without providing any specific feedback on what the employee needs to do to improve. This feedback is not helpful because it does not provide the employee with clear direction on what they need to do differently.

Without specific feedback, the employee may not understand what they need to do to improve or may become frustrated and disengaged. They may also feel that the feedback is unfair or irrelevant, which can damage the relationship between the employee and the manager.

Ineffective feedback can also occur when it is delivered in a negative or critical manner, without any recognition of the employee's strengths or contributions. This can leave the employee feeling demotivated and discouraged, and may lead to decreased job satisfaction and commitment to the organization.

Overall, ineffective feedback can be damaging to both the employee and the organization, as it can lead to confusion, frustration, and disengagement. It is important for managers to provide specific, actionable feedback that recognizes employees' strengths and provides guidance for improvement. This can help employees feel valued and supported, and can lead to increased engagement, job satisfaction, and commitment.

An example of inappropriate feedback for leaders of color is when feedback is based on stereotypes or assumptions about their race, ethnicity, or cultural background.

For instance, a manager may provide feedback to a Black leader that they are "too aggressive" or "too emotional," based on stereotypes that are associated with Black people. This feedback is inappropriate because it is based on assumptions about the leader's behavior, rather than their actual performance.

Similarly, a manager may provide feedback to an Asian leader that they are "too quiet" or "too passive," based on stereotypes about Asian people. This feedback is also inappropriate because it is based on assumptions about the leader's behavior, rather than their actual performance.

Feedback that is based on stereotypes or assumptions can be damaging to leaders of color, as it can reinforce negative stereotypes and undermine their confidence and credibility. It can also lead to a sense of isolation and marginalization, as leaders of color may feel that they are not being evaluated based on their actual performance.

Overall, feedback for leaders of color should be based on objective, specific, and actionable criteria, rather than stereotypes or assumptions about their race, ethnicity, or cultural background. This can help ensure that leaders of color are evaluated fairly and can be successful in their roles.

There are several models for feedback that can be effective in different situations. One popular model is the "SBI" model, which stands for Situation, Behavior, Impact. Here's how it works:

1. Situation: Start by describing the situation or context in which the behavior you want to address occurred. This helps provide context and ensures that both parties are on the same page.

2. Behavior: Describe the behavior you want to address, using specific, objective language. Avoid generalizations or personal attacks, and focus on the specific actions or behaviors that need to change.

3. Impact: Describe the impact of the behavior on the individual, the team, or the organization. This helps the recipient understand the consequences of their actions and why it's important to change.

For example, using the SBI model, a manager might say:

"During yesterday's team meeting (Situation), I noticed that you interrupted other team members several times while they were speaking (Behavior). This made some team members feel frustrated and talked over, and may have prevented us from fully exploring some important ideas (Impact)."

The SBI model is effective because it focuses on specific behaviors and their impact, rather than personal attacks or generalizations. It helps ensure that feedback is objective and constructive, and that the recipient understands why the behavior needs to change.

Another model that can be effective is the "STAR" model, which stands for Situation, Task, Action, Result. This model is particularly useful for providing positive feedback and recognizing achievements. It involves describing a situation or task, the action taken, and the positive result that was achieved.

Ultimately, the most important thing is to tailor the feedback model to the specific situation and to focus on specific behaviors or actions that need to be addressed. By providing clear, constructive feedback, individuals and organizations can improve their performance and achieve their goals.

When feedback goes wrong, it can have negative consequences for both the giver and the recipient of the feedback, as well as for the broader organizational culture. Here are some of the potential consequences of ineffective or poorly delivered feedback:

- ***Demotivation:*** If feedback is overly critical, vague, or delivered in an unconstructive manner, it can demotivate the recipient and decrease their engagement and job satisfaction.
- ***Defensive behavior:*** If feedback is perceived as unfair or unjustified, it can lead to defensive behavior, where the recipient becomes resistant to feedback and less receptive to future suggestions.
- ***Damage to relationships:*** If feedback is delivered in a confrontational or accusatory manner, it can damage relationships between colleagues or between a manager and their direct reports.
- ***Decreased performance:*** If feedback is not actionable or focused on the wrong areas, it can lead to decreased performance and a lack of progress towards organizational goals.
- ***Negative organizational culture:*** If feedback is not seen as a positive and constructive process, it can lead to a negative organizational culture where employees feel undervalued and unsupported.

To prevent these negative consequences, it is important to ensure that feedback is delivered in a constructive and supportive manner, with a focus on specific behaviors or actions that need to be addressed. Feedback should be tailored to the individual and their specific goals, and delivered in a way that is timely, specific, and actionable.

Additionally, feedback should be seen as a positive and constructive process that supports individual and organizational growth, rather than a punitive or negative process. By delivering feedback effectively, individuals and organizations can improve their performance, strengthen relationships, and create a positive and supportive organizational culture.

Poor Performance

Addressing poor performance through feedback is essential for both the individual and the organization. It promotes improvement, accountability, organizational success, fairness, and professional growth, ultimately leading to a positive and supportive work environment.

During the initial stages of my leadership voyage, a compelling assertion that struck a chord with me was, "Your judgment is significantly influenced by the extent of incompetence you tolerate over time." This statement underscores the necessity of actively recognizing and assisting those who may be facing challenges. Offering feedback is an investment in your employees, and every instance in which you decide not to address a performance or behavior issue erodes the equity you initially invested in them upon hiring.

Providing feedback on poor performance enables individuals to understand where they are falling short and what specific areas they need to improve. By identifying these areas, individuals can develop a plan to address their weaknesses and enhance their performance.

By addressing issues in a timely manner, you not only create an environment of accountability and growth but also demonstrate that you value and support your employees' development. A leader's ability to recognize and address incompetence is crucial for the overall success of the team and the organization. It fosters a culture of continuous improvement and creates a workforce that is both resilient and adaptable in the face of challenges. So, remember that your leadership will be defined not only by the successes you achieve but also by the way you handle and support the growth of your employees.

Accountability is another important aspect of providing feedback on poor performance.

Feedback makes individuals aware of the expectations for their role and motivates them to meet those expectations. This sense of responsibility can lead to better performance and higher job satisfaction.

Organizational success is also impacted by addressing poor performance through feedback. When individuals improve their performance, the organization as a whole benefits, allowing it to achieve its goals and objectives more effectively.

Fairness plays a crucial role in providing feedback about poor performance. By being transparent about expectations and areas needing improvement, individuals have the opportunity to understand their current standing and work towards better performance, rather than being caught off-guard by negative consequences or criticism.

Lastly, professional growth is fostered through feedback on poor performance. As individuals address their weaknesses, they can develop new skills, improve their performance, and become more valuable members of the organization.

While improvement and growth are related concepts, they differ in their focus and scope. Improvement is centered on addressing specific weaknesses or challenges to become more proficient in a particular area, whereas growth involves the overall development and expansion of an individual's skills, knowledge, and abilities. Growth is often focused on long-term personal and professional development, encompassing a wider range of experiences and challenges.

Both improvement and growth are crucial for personal and professional development, contributing to success in the workplace and in life. By embracing feedback, individuals can work towards continuous improvement and growth, ultimately benefiting both themselves and the organizations they are a part of.

Key Questions

How can feedback based on stereotypes or assumptions negatively impact leaders of color?

Feedback based on stereotypes or assumptions can negatively impact leaders of color by reinforcing negative stereotypes, undermining their confidence and credibility, and leading to feelings of isolation and marginalization. This can result in leaders of color feeling that they are not being evaluated fairly and based on their actual performance.

What are the key principles for providing fair and objective feedback to leaders of color?

Key principles for providing fair and objective feedback to leaders of color include basing feedback on specific, objective, and actionable criteria rather than stereotypes or assumptions about their race, ethnicity, or cultural background. This ensures that leaders of color are evaluated fairly and can be successful in their roles.

What is the SBI model of feedback, and why is it effective?

The SBI model of feedback stands for Situation, Behavior, Impact. It is effective because it focuses on specific behaviors and their impact, rather than personal attacks or generalizations. By describing the situation, behavior, and impact, it ensures that feedback is objective, constructive, and helps the recipient understand why the behavior needs to change.

Can you explain the STAR model for providing positive feedback and recognizing achievements?

The STAR model for providing positive feedback and recognizing achievements stands for Situation, Task, Action, Result. This model involves describing a situation or task, the action taken, and the positive result that was achieved. It helps to highlight accomplishments and reinforce positive behavior.

What are the potential negative consequences of ineffective or poorly delivered feedback?

Potential negative consequences of ineffective or poorly delivered feedback include demotivation, defensive behavior, damage to relationships, decreased performance, and a negative organizational culture.

How can constructive and supportive feedback delivery prevent these negative consequences?

Constructive and supportive feedback delivery can prevent these negative consequences by focusing on specific behaviors or actions that need to be addressed, tailoring feedback to the individual and their goals, and delivering feedback in a timely, specific, and actionable manner. This promotes a positive and constructive process that supports individual and organizational growth.

How does addressing poor performance through feedback benefit both the individual and the organization?

Addressing poor performance through feedback benefits both the individual and the organization by promoting improvement, accountability, organizational success, fairness, and professional growth. This creates a positive and supportive work environment that fosters continuous development.

What is the difference between improvement and growth in the context of personal and professional development?

The difference between improvement and growth in the context of personal and professional development lies in their focus and scope. Improvement is centered on addressing specific weaknesses or challenges, while growth involves the overall development and expansion of an individual's skills, knowledge, and abilities, often focused on long-term personal and professional development.

Key Questions (cont.)

How do improvement and growth contribute to success in the workplace and in life?

Improvement and growth contribute to success in the workplace and in life by allowing individuals to continually develop their skills, adapt to new challenges, and take on new responsibilities. This enables them to become more effective and valuable members of their organizations and achieve personal fulfillment.

Why is it important for leaders to address incompetence and support the growth of their employees?

It is important for leaders to address incompetence and support the growth of their employees because doing so fosters a culture of continuous improvement, creates a workforce that is resilient and adaptable to challenges, and contributes to the overall success of the team and the organization. By addressing incompetence proactively, leaders demonstrate that they value and support their employees' development, ultimately benefiting both the employees and the organization as a whole.

Investments: Cybernetics

Practice 8.1

Case Scenario
EchoTech Company

EcoTech is a rapidly growing green technology company located in the city of Greenfield. Despite its success, the company has been facing high employee turnover and burnout. In response, the management team has decided to apply an ecological framework to analyze and improve the workplace conditions for their employees.

Background
Greenfield is known for its culturally diverse population and progressive values. However, the city has been grappling with issues related to discrimination and gentrification. These broader cultural and societal factors have seeped into the workplace, impacting the well-being and productivity of EcoTech's employees.

Complicated Factors

Physical Environment: The company's office building is an old factory converted into a modern workspace. While it has an appealing aesthetic, the building suffers from poor ventilation, insufficient natural light, and noise pollution.

Social Relationships: The company has a mix of employees from various cultural backgrounds, and some employees have reported feeling isolated or excluded due to language barriers or cultural differences. Moreover, the competitive work culture has led to strained relationships between team members and departments.

Organizational Policies and Practices: EcoTech has been focusing on rapid growth, leading to long working hours and a lack of work-life balance. Employees also report dissatisfaction with the lack of training and development opportunities and unclear career progression paths.

Investments: Cybernetics

Broader Cultural and Societal Factors: Greenfield's issues related to discrimination and gentrification have also affected EcoTech's workforce. Some employees have faced prejudice, both within the company and the broader community, while others have been struggling with the rising cost of living due to gentrification.

1. How has the city of Greenfield's cultural diversity and progressive values influenced EcoTech's workplace environment?

2. How do the broader cultural and societal factors, such as discrimination and gentrification, impact EcoTech's employees?

3. How do the physical environment challenges, including poor ventilation, insufficient natural light, and noise pollution, affect employee well-being and productivity at EcoTech?

4. What specific social relationship issues are faced by employees at EcoTech, and how do these issues contribute to high employee turnover and burnout?

5. How do EcoTech's organizational policies and practices, particularly those related to rapid growth, contribute to employee dissatisfaction and work-life imbalance?

6. What are some potential solutions for improving the physical environment at EcoTech's office building?

7. How can EcoTech address the social relationship challenges among its culturally diverse workforce and promote a more inclusive and collaborative work culture?

8. What changes can EcoTech implement in its organizational policies and practices to improve employee satisfaction and retention, particularly regarding work-life balance, training and development opportunities, and career progression paths?

9. How can EcoTech actively address broader cultural and societal factors, such as discrimination and gentrification, both within the company and in the Greenfield community?

Practice 8.1 (cont.)

10. How might addressing these complicated factors and applying an ecological framework help reduce employee turnover, burnout, and ultimately, improve productivity at EcoTech?

Practice 8.2

Group Activity
Role-Playing Feedback Scenarios with a Focus on Fair Evaluation

Objective:
To practice providing constructive feedback that is objective, specific, and actionable, while avoiding stereotypes or assumptions about race, ethnicity, or cultural background.

Materials
- Printed or digital copies of various feedback scenarios
- Timer

Instructions
- Divide participants into pairs, designating one person as the manager and the other as the employee.
- Provide each pair with a scenario that requires the manager to give feedback to the employee. These scenarios should involve situations where there might be a risk of stereotype-based feedback, and emphasize the importance of fair evaluations for leaders of color.
- Instruct the manager to use either the "SBI" (Situation, Behavior, Impact) or "STAR" (Situation, Task, Action, Result) model to provide feedback, keeping it objective, specific, and actionable. Encourage them to focus on the behavior or action rather than the individual's race, ethnicity, or cultural background.
- Allow each pair 5-10 minutes to practice their feedback scenario, with the manager delivering the feedback and the employee responding.
- After completing the scenario, have the pairs switch roles and repeat the process with a new scenario.
- Once all pairs have completed both scenarios, bring the group together to debrief. Discuss what worked well, what challenges were encountered, and any insights gained from practicing these feedback models.

Practice 8.2 (cont.)

- Encourage participants to reflect on the importance of providing fair and objective feedback to leaders of color, the potential consequences of ineffective or poorly delivered feedback, and how these models can be applied in their own work environments.

By engaging in this activity, participants can build their skills in providing constructive feedback that supports fair evaluation for leaders of color, while avoiding stereotype-based judgments. This practice will help to foster a more inclusive and equitable work environment for all employees.

INVESTMENTS: CYBERNETICS

Practice 8.3

Group Activity
Effective Feedback for a Diverse Workforce

Objective:
This large group activity aims to teach participants the importance of providing effective and inclusive feedback in the workplace, helping them understand how to deliver feedback that is timely, specific, and actionable.

Duration   2 Hours

Materials

- Flipchart or whiteboard
- Markers
- Sticky notes
- Handout on effective feedback, ineffective feedback, and inappropriate feedback for leaders of color (based on the provided text)
- Case study scenarios (optional)

Activity Outline

1. Introduction (10 minutes)
   - Begin with a brief introduction to the importance of feedback in the workplace.
   - Discuss the impact of feedback on employee retention, job satisfaction, and commitment.
   - Provide an overview of the learning activity and its objectives.

2. Understanding Effective Feedback (20 minutes)
   - Divide participants into small groups.
   - Distribute the handout on effective feedback, ineffective feedback, and inappropriate feedback for leaders of color.
   - Ask participants to read the handout and discuss their understanding of effective feedback.
   - Reconvene and ask each group to share their insights with the larger group.

3. Identifying Ineffective and Inappropriate Feedback (20 minutes)
    - Lead a discussion on the characteristics of ineffective and inappropriate feedback.
    - Present examples from the handout, and ask participants to identify what makes the feedback ineffective or inappropriate.
    - Optional: Use case study scenarios to engage participants in analyzing various feedback situations.
    - Discuss the consequences of providing ineffective or inappropriate feedback.

4. Role-Playing Exercise: Providing Effective and Inclusive Feedback (40 minutes)
    - Divide participants into pairs or small groups.
    - Assign each pair or group a role-playing scenario that involves providing feedback (e.g., a manager giving feedback to an employee, a team member giving feedback to a peer).
    - Instruct participants to practice providing effective and inclusive feedback, based on the principles discussed earlier.
    - Allow each pair or group to role-play their scenario, with the rest of the participants observing and providing feedback.
    - Discuss the lessons learned from the role-playing exercise.

5. Developing Strategies for Effective and Inclusive Feedback (20 minutes)
    - Ask participants to brainstorm strategies for providing effective and inclusive feedback in the workplace.
    - Encourage participants to share their ideas and experiences.
    - Facilitate a discussion on best practices for providing feedback that is timely, specific, actionable, and sensitive to diversity and inclusion.

6. Action Plan (10 minutes)
    - Ask participants to reflect on what they've learned and create a personal action plan to improve their feedback skills in the workplace.
    - Encourage participants to write down three specific actions they will take to provide more effective and inclusive feedback.
    - Have participants share their action plans with a partner or small group for feedback and accountability.

7. Closing (10 minutes)
   - Reconvene the large group and ask for volunteers to share their action plans.
   - Summarize the key takeaways from the learning activity.
   - Encourage participants to put their action plans into practice and continue the conversation with their colleagues and leaders.

Intersectional Leadership: Building Resilient Workforces

Answer Key 8.1

1. Greenfield's cultural diversity and progressive values have influenced EcoTech's workplace environment by attracting a diverse workforce. This diversity can foster innovation and creativity but also presents challenges, such as language barriers and cultural differences, which can contribute to feelings of isolation or exclusion among employees.

2. Broader cultural and societal factors, such as discrimination and gentrification, impact EcoTech's employees by creating a hostile environment for some, leading to prejudice both within the company and in the community. Gentrification can also make it difficult for employees to afford housing, adding financial stress to their lives.

3. The physical environment challenges at EcoTech, including poor ventilation, insufficient natural light, and noise pollution, can negatively impact employee well-being and productivity by causing discomfort, increasing stress levels, and making it difficult for employees to concentrate on their work.

4. Specific social relationship issues faced by employees at EcoTech include feelings of isolation or exclusion due to language barriers or cultural differences, as well as strained relationships between team members and departments resulting from the competitive work culture. These issues can contribute to high employee turnover and burnout by making employees feel unsupported and disconnected from their colleagues.

5. EcoTech's organizational policies and practices related to rapid growth contribute to employee dissatisfaction and work-life imbalance by demanding long working hours, leading to burnout and a lack of work-life balance. Additionally, the lack of training and development opportunities and unclear career progression paths can leave employees feeling undervalued and unsure about their future within the company.

6. Potential solutions for improving the physical environment at EcoTech's office building include addressing ventilation issues, maximizing natural light through window installations or light shelves, and implementing noise reduction measures, such as sound-absorbing panels or white noise machines.

7. EcoTech can address social relationship challenges among its culturally diverse workforce and promote a more inclusive and collaborative work culture by providing cultural sensitivity training, organizing team-building activities, and creating opportunities for employees to connect across language and cultural barriers.

8. Changes EcoTech can implement in its organizational policies and practices to improve employee satisfaction and retention include introducing flexible work arrangements, providing training and development opportunities, and implementing transparent career progression guidelines that offer employees a clear path for growth within the company.

9. EcoTech can actively address broader cultural and societal factors, such as discrimination and gentrification, both within the company and in the Greenfield community by creating and enforcing policies that promote diversity, equity, and inclusion, as well as partnering with local community organizations to support initiatives that combat discrimination and gentrification.

INVESTMENTS: CYBERNETICS

10. Addressing these complicated factors and applying an ecological framework can help reduce employee turnover and burnout at EcoTech by creating a more supportive and inclusive work environment that prioritizes employee well-being. By addressing the underlying issues that contribute to dissatisfaction, the company can ultimately improve productivity and retain its talented workforce.

"Future Ready"

BeanTime had historically struggled to attract and retain diverse talent at the leadership level, and recognized that a lack of diversity in leadership was hindering its ability to compete and innovate.

To address this issue, the company launched a comprehensive succession planning initiative focused on identifying and developing diverse leaders. The initiative began with an assessment of the current talent pool, and identified several high-potential employees from diverse backgrounds who were seen as potential candidates for leadership roles.

These individuals were then enrolled in a leadership development program that included mentorship, coaching, and training on key leadership competencies. The program was designed to help these employees build the skills and experience they needed to succeed in leadership roles, while also providing them with the support and guidance they needed to navigate the challenges of corporate culture.

Over time, several of the employees who participated in the program were promoted into key leadership positions within the company. These individuals brought diverse perspectives and experiences to their roles, and helped to drive innovation and growth within the organization.

As a result of this initiative, the company was able to significantly increase the diversity of its leadership ranks, and to create a more inclusive and supportive culture for employees from diverse backgrounds. The success of the initiative also helped to position the company as a leader in promoting diversity and inclusion in the financial services industry.

Overall, this story demonstrates the power of succession planning to promote diversity and inclusion in leadership. By identifying and developing diverse talent, organizations can create more inclusive cultures, drive innovation and growth, and position themselves for long-term success.

Chapter 9
Succession Planning

The origin of succession planning can be traced back to ancient civilizations and their systems of selecting and preparing successors for leadership positions. In ancient Egypt, Africa, Rome, and China, the practice of succession planning was primarily focused on ensuring the continuity of leadership, particularly in royal or imperial families, to maintain stability and order in society.

In more modern times, the concept of succession planning emerged in the early 20th century in the business world. As companies grew larger and more complex, the need for a structured approach to identifying and grooming potential leaders for key positions became increasingly important. This was particularly true for family-owned businesses, where the succession of leadership from one generation to the next was a critical concern.

Over time, succession planning has evolved into a formalized process that focuses not only on identifying potential successors for leadership roles but also on providing them with the necessary training, development, and mentorship to prepare them for the responsibilities that come with the position. Today, succession planning is widely recognized as a crucial component of effective human resource management and organizational strategy.

The first step in succession planning is to identify the key positions within the organization that are critical to the success of the business. These positions may include senior leadership roles, key technical or operational roles, or other critical positions.

Identifying key positions for promotions at work means identifying the roles within an organization that are critical to the success of the business and that have the greatest impact on achieving the organization's goals. These roles may include leadership positions, technical or operational roles, or other positions that are critical to the organization's core functions.

Identifying key positions is an important part of succession planning and talent management. By identifying the roles that are most critical to the organization's success, organizations can ensure that they are investing in the development of employees who have the potential to fill these roles in the future.

When identifying key positions, organizations may consider factors such as:
- The level of impact the role has on achieving the organization's goals
- The complexity of the role and the level of skill and expertise required
- The level of visibility and responsibility associated with the role
- The degree of alignment between the role and the organization's core values and mission
- The potential for the role to evolve and grow over time

Assessment

Once key positions have been identified, organizations can begin to develop talent pipelines and succession plans for these roles. This may involve identifying high-potential employees who have the skills, experience, and potential to fill these roles in the future, and investing in their development through training, mentoring, coaching, and other programs.

The next step is to assess the talent that is currently within the organization. This may involve evaluating employees based on their skills, experience, performance, and potential for growth. Talent assessment is a critical part of talent management and is used to identify high-potential employees, develop career plans, and make decisions about promotions, job assignments, and other talent-related issues.

Talent assessment can take many forms and may involve various methods such as:

- Performance reviews: These are formal evaluations of an employee's performance against established job expectations and goals.
- Competency assessments: These are assessments of an employee's knowledge, skills, and abilities related to specific job functions or competencies.
- Behavioral assessments: These are assessments of an employee's personality traits, work style, and interpersonal skills.
- 360-degree feedback: This is a process of gathering feedback from an employee's supervisor, peers, and subordinates to provide a comprehensive view of their strengths and weaknesses.
- Succession planning assessments: These are assessments of an employee's potential to move into higher-level roles in the organization.

Talent assessment is an ongoing process that involves regular feedback and communication with employees. It is important for organizations to create a culture of continuous learning and development, where employees are encouraged to seek feedback, set goals, and pursue opportunities for growth and development.

Talent assessment is an important part of talent management and can help organizations to identify and develop the talent they need to achieve their goals and drive long-term success.

IDENTIFY KEY SKILLS

Identifying potential leaders is a critical part of talent management, and there are several key strategies that can help you to identify employees with leadership potential.

First, look for demonstrated skills and behaviors. Identify employees who have demonstrated leadership skills and behaviors in their current or past roles. Look for employees who have taken on leadership responsibilities, mentored others, or shown initiative and innovation in their work.

Next, assess performance and potential by conducting performance reviews and assessments to evaluate employees' performance and potential. Look for employees who consistently exceed expectations and show a strong potential for growth and development.

Another strategy is to solicit feedback from others. Seek feedback from colleagues, supervisors, and other stakeholders who work closely with employees. Ask for their input on employees' leadership potential and gather feedback on their strengths, areas for improvement, and potential for growth.

It is also important to look for passion and commitment. Identify employees who are passionate about their work and committed to the organization's goals and values. Look for employees who take ownership of their work and demonstrate a strong work ethic and commitment to excellence.

Finally, provide development opportunities. Offer employees opportunities for development and growth, such as training programs, mentorship, or stretch assignments. Look for employees who take advantage of these opportunities and show a willingness to learn and grow.

Identifying potential leaders requires a combination of assessment, observation, and feedback. By focusing on employees who demonstrate the skills, behaviors, and qualities of effective leaders, and providing them with opportunities for development and growth, you can help to build a strong pipeline of future leaders for your organization.

In addition to identifying potential leaders, it is crucial to plan for transitions. As potential leaders are identified and developed, the organization can begin to plan for transitions. This may involve creating a plan for how employees will be promoted or moved into new roles when they become available, and how they will be supported during the transition process.

Successfully onboarding new employees means providing them with a smooth and seamless transition into the organization, setting them up for success in their new role, and helping them to integrate into the organizational culture.

To achieve this, provide clear communication to new employees about their role, responsibilities, and expectations. This includes providing them with an overview of the organization's culture, values, and goals, as well as any policies or procedures they need to be aware of.

Offer a structured orientation program that includes information about the organization, their role, and any training they need to complete. This can help them to get up to speed quickly and feel more confident in their new role.

Ensure new employees have the support and resources they need to be successful in their new role. This includes providing them with access to tools, equipment, and software they need, as well as a mentor or buddy who can help them navigate the organization and answer questions.

Provide regular feedback and check-ins to ensure new employees are adjusting well to their new role and to identify any areas where they may need additional support or training.

Finally, help new employees integrate into the organizational culture by introducing them to key stakeholders, encouraging them to participate in social events, and providing opportunities for them to connect with colleagues. By successfully onboarding new employees, organizations can help them to feel more engaged and committed to their new role, reduce turnover, and increase overall productivity and performance.

Monitor Progress

The organization should monitor the progress of its succession planning efforts and make adjustments as needed. This may involve regularly assessing the performance of potential leaders, identifying new talent as it emerges, and making changes to development programs as needed.

Monitoring the progress of succession planning is important because it helps organizations to ensure that they are developing and retaining the talent they need to succeed in the long term.

Identifying gaps and areas for improvement is one reason why monitoring progress is essential.

Monitoring the progress of succession planning can help organizations identify any gaps or areas where they need to improve their talent development strategies. This can include identifying areas where there are skill or knowledge gaps, or where there are not enough diverse candidates in the pipeline.

Ensuring alignment with business goals is another reason why monitoring progress is crucial. Monitoring progress can help organizations ensure that their succession planning efforts are aligned with their overall business goals and objectives. By tracking progress and making adjustments as needed, organizations can ensure that they are developing the talent they need to achieve their strategic priorities.

Improving retention and engagement is an additional benefit of monitoring progress. By monitoring progress and communicating with employees about their development and career opportunities, organizations can improve employee retention and engagement. Employees who feel that they have a clear path for growth and development are more likely to stay with the organization and be motivated to perform at a high level.

Lastly, monitoring progress can help organizations increase diversity and inclusion by identifying areas where they need to improve their recruitment and development strategies. By tracking the progress of diverse candidates and making adjustments as needed, organizations can ensure that they are developing a pipeline of talent that reflects the diversity of their workforce and the communities they serve.

Monitoring the progress of succession planning is critical for organizations that want to develop and retain the talent they need to succeed in the long term. By tracking progress and making adjustments as needed, organizations can ensure that they are building a strong pipeline of future leaders and that they are aligned with their overall business goals and objectives.

Succession planning is an important process for ensuring that an organization has the talent and leadership it needs to succeed both now and in the future. By identifying and developing potential leaders and planning for transitions, organizations can create a pipeline of talent that is ready to take on new challenges and drive growth and success.

The 9-Box Model

There are several models for succession planning, but one popular model is the 9-Box Model. The 9-Box Model was presented by McKinsey & Company, a global management consulting firm, in the late 1960s. The model was designed to help organizations assess the potential of their employees for future leadership roles and to identify those who were ready for promotion.

Since then, the 9-Box Model has become a widely used tool for succession planning and talent management in organizations of all sizes and industries. While the exact origins of the model are not clear, it is generally attributed to McKinsey & Company and its consultants.

The model is typically displayed as a 3x3 grid, with one axis representing an employee's potential (i.e., their ability to take on more responsibility and perform at a higher level) and the other axis representing their performance (i.e., how well they are currently performing in their role). Each box in the grid represents a different level of potential and performance, ranging from high potential/high performance (top right box) to low potential/low performance (bottom left box).

Using the 9-Box Model, organizations can identify employees who are high potential/high performers and ensure they are being groomed for future leadership roles. They can also identify employees who may need additional development or support to improve their performance or potential.

The 9-Box Model is a popular model for succession planning because it is simple to understand and easy to use. It can also be customized to fit the specific needs of different organizations, and it can be used to assess the potential of employees at all levels of the organization, from entry-level to senior leadership positions.

Innovation School District is a large urban school district that has been experiencing rapid growth in recent years. The district is committed to developing its employees and building a strong pipeline of future leaders, and it has decided to use the 9-Box Model to assess the potential of its employees for future leadership roles.

To begin the process, Innovation School District gathers data on each of its employees' performance and potential, using a variety of sources including performance reviews, feedback from managers, and assessments. The district then creates a 9-Box grid, with the horizontal axis representing potential and the vertical axis representing performance.

Using the grid, Innovation School District identifies employees who fall into each of the nine boxes. For example, employees who are high potential and high performers are placed in the top right box, while employees who are low potential and low performers are placed in the bottom left box.

Once the employees have been placed in the appropriate boxes, Innovation School District analyzes the results to identify trends and opportunities. The district identifies employees who are high potential but may need additional development or support to improve their performance, as well as employees who are high performers but may not have the potential for future leadership roles.

Based on the results of the 9-Box Model, Innovation School District develops a talent management plan that includes targeted development programs for high-potential employees, as well as plans to recruit and hire employees with the potential for future leadership roles. The company also uses the 9-Box Model on an ongoing basis to monitor the progress of its employees and ensure that it is building a strong pipeline of future leaders.

KEY QUESTIONS

What is the origin of succession planning?

The origin of succession planning can be traced back to ancient civilizations such as Egypt, Rome, and China, where the focus was on ensuring continuity of leadership in royal or imperial families. In modern times, the concept emerged in the early 20th century in the business world, evolving into a formalized process that focuses on identifying potential successors and providing them with necessary training, development, and mentorship.

Why is identifying key positions important in succession planning?

Identifying key positions is crucial in succession planning and talent management because it helps organizations invest in the development of employees with the potential to fill these critical roles in the future. By focusing on roles most critical to the organization's success, organizations can ensure they are building a strong talent pipeline for the future.

What factors should be considered when identifying key positions?

Factors to consider when identifying key positions include the role's impact on achieving the organization's goals, the complexity of the role and the level of skill and expertise required, the visibility and responsibility associated with the role, the degree of alignment between the role and the organization's core values and mission, and the potential for the role to evolve and grow over time.

What is the purpose of talent assessment in succession planning?

Talent assessment is a critical part of succession planning and is used to identify high-potential employees, develop career plans, and make decisions about promotions, job assignments, and other talent-related issues. It helps organizations identify and develop the talent they need to achieve their goals and drive long-term success.

What are some methods used in talent assessment?

Talent assessment methods include performance reviews, competency assessments, behavioral assessments, 360-degree feedback, and succession planning assessments. These methods help provide a comprehensive view of employees' strengths and weaknesses, allowing organizations to make informed decisions about their talent management strategies.

How can organizations support high-potential employees in their development?

Organizations can support high-potential employees through various development initiatives, such as training programs, mentorship, coaching, stretch assignments, and opportunities for cross-functional collaboration. These initiatives help employees acquire new skills, broaden their perspectives, and prepare for future leadership roles.

Why is monitoring the progress of succession planning important?

Monitoring the progress of succession planning is important because it helps organizations ensure they are developing and retaining the talent needed for long-term success. By tracking progress and making adjustments as needed, organizations can identify gaps, ensure alignment with business goals, improve retention and engagement, and increase diversity and inclusion.

How can organizations effectively onboard new leaders as part of their succession planning efforts?

Effective onboarding of new leaders involves clear communication about their roles and responsibilities, a structured orientation program, provision of support and resources, regular feedback and check-ins, and integration into the organizational culture. These elements help new leaders feel more engaged and committed to their roles, reduce turnover, and increase overall productivity and performance.

Key Questions (cont.)

How can organizations ensure that their succession planning efforts promote diversity and inclusion?

Organizations can promote diversity and inclusion in their succession planning by actively seeking out diverse talent, implementing unbiased assessment and selection processes, providing equal access to development opportunities, and fostering a culture that values diverse perspectives and backgrounds.

What role does organizational culture play in succession planning?

Organizational culture plays a significant role in succession planning, as it influences employees' engagement, motivation, and commitment to the organization. A supportive and inclusive culture that values continuous learning, development, and growth can help organizations retain and develop high-potential employees, ultimately ensuring a strong pipeline of future leaders.

Practice 9.1

Innovation School District has recently hired a new superintendent, Dr. Anderson, who is committed to ensuring the district's continued growth and success. She has heard about the 9-Box Model and believes it could be a valuable tool in identifying and developing the district's future leaders. Dr. Anderson has decided to hold a meeting with her executive team to discuss implementing the 9-Box Model as part of the district's succession planning process.

Meeting Participants

- Dr. Anderson, Superintendent
- Mr. Thompson, Assistant Superintendent
- Ms. Johnson, Director of Human Resources
- Mr. Garcia, Director of Curriculum and Instruction
- Ms. Kim, Director of Finance

Dr. Anderson: Thank you all for joining me today. As you know, our district has been experiencing rapid growth, and it's essential that we have a strong pipeline of future leaders to ensure our continued success. I believe the 9-Box Model could be a valuable tool in identifying and developing our future leaders. I'd like to hear your thoughts on implementing this model in our district.

Mr. Thompson: I agree, Dr. Anderson. The 9-Box Model is a straightforward and efficient way to assess our employees' potential and performance. It can help us identify high-potential employees who may need additional development and support, as well as high performers who may not have the potential for future leadership roles.

Ms. Johnson: I think the 9-Box Model could be a great addition to our talent management strategy. In Human Resources, we can gather the necessary data, such as performance reviews and feedback from managers, to create the 9-Box grid. We can then work with each department to analyze the results and develop targeted development programs for our high-potential employees.

PRACTICE 9.1 (CONT.)

Mr. Garcia: I agree that the 9-Box Model could be a valuable tool for our district. However, I think it's important that we also consider other factors, such as an employee's commitment to our district's values and goals, when assessing their potential for future leadership roles.

Ms. Kim: That's a good point, Mr. Garcia. We can customize the 9-Box Model to include additional criteria that are important to our district, such as alignment with our values and goals. This would provide a more comprehensive assessment of our employees' potential for future leadership roles.

Dr. Anderson: Thank you all for your input. It seems like we all agree that implementing the 9-Box Model could be beneficial for our district. Ms. Johnson, please work with your team in Human Resources to gather the necessary data and create the 9-Box grid. Once that is completed, we'll schedule another meeting to review the results and discuss our next steps in developing a talent management plan.

In this scenario, Innovation School District's leadership team recognizes the potential benefits of using the 9-Box Model for succession planning. They discuss its implementation and agree to move forward with the process. By using the 9-Box Model and customizing it to fit their specific needs, Innovation School District can better identify and develop future leaders, ensuring the district's continued growth and success.

1. How will the executive team ensure that the 9-Box Model is implemented consistently across all departments within Innovation School District?

2. What specific criteria will be used to determine an employee's potential and performance in the 9-Box Model?

3. How often will the 9-Box Model be utilized to assess employees and update the talent management plan?

4. What resources will be made available to help high-potential employees develop their skills and prepare for future leadership roles?

5. How will the executive team address potential concerns or resistance from employees about the implementation of the 9-Box Model?

6. How will Innovation School District track the success of the 9-Box Model implementation and its impact on succession planning?

7. In what ways can the 9-Box Model be adapted to better align with the specific needs and values of Innovation School District?

8. How will the district ensure that the process remains transparent and objective, avoiding biases in the assessment of employees?

9. What measures will be put in place to ensure employee confidentiality during the 9-Box Model assessment process?

10. How will Innovation School District communicate the implementation of the 9-Box Model and its benefits to employees throughout the district?

INTERSECTIONAL LEADERSHIP: BUILDING RESILIENT WORKFORCES

Practice 9.2

Group Activity
Strengthening the Leadership Pipeline through Succession Planning

Objective:
This activity aims to help senior leadership identify key positions within the organization and develop a strategic approach to succession planning, ensuring a strong pipeline of leaders for the future.

Duration   2 Hours

Materials
- Flipchart or whiteboard
- Markers
- Sticky notes
- Handout on succession planning, key position identification, and talent development

Activity Outline

1. Introduction (15 minutes)
   - Begin with a brief introduction to the importance of succession planning and its historical context.
   - Discuss how succession planning has evolved over time and its role in modern organizations.
   - Provide an overview of the learning activity and its objectives.

2. Identifying Key Positions (30 minutes)
   - Divide participants into small groups.
   - Distribute the handout on succession planning, key position identification, and talent development.
   - Ask participants to read the handout and discuss the factors to consider when identifying key positions within the organization.
   - Instruct each group to identify key positions within their organization, based on the factors discussed in the handout.
   - Reconvene and ask each group to share their identified key positions with the larger group.

3. Talent Development Strategies (45 minutes)
    - Lead a discussion on various talent development strategies that can be used to prepare potential successors for key positions.
    - Strategies may include mentoring, coaching, job rotations, training programs, and stretch assignments.
    - Ask each group to brainstorm specific talent development strategies they can implement in their organization to prepare potential successors for the identified key positions.
    - Reconvene and ask each group to share their strategies with the larger group.

4. Succession Planning Action Plan (20 minutes)
    - Instruct participants to create an action plan for implementing their identified talent development strategies and strengthening their leadership pipeline.
    - Encourage participants to consider the resources, timelines, and potential obstacles in implementing their action plans.
    - Ask participants to share their action plans with a partner or small group for feedback and accountability.

5. Closing (10 minutes)
    - Reconvene the large group and ask for volunteers to share their action plans.
    - Summarize the key takeaways from the learning activity.
    - Encourage participants to put their action plans into practice and continue the conversation with their colleagues and leaders to ensure the organization's leadership pipeline remains strong.

Answer Key 9.1

1. The executive team will ensure consistent implementation of the 9-Box Model by developing clear guidelines and providing training for all departments. They will also assign a team, led by the Human Resources department, to oversee the process and ensure that all departments follow the established procedures.
2. The specific criteria used to determine an employee's potential and performance in the 9-Box Model will include factors such as job performance, leadership capabilities, ability to learn and adapt, alignment with district values, and commitment to the district's goals.
3. The 9-Box Model will be utilized annually to assess employees and update the talent management plan, allowing for regular review and adjustments based on employee development and changes within the district.
4. Resources made available for high-potential employees may include training programs, workshops, mentorship opportunities, job rotations, and targeted development plans tailored to each individual's needs and goals.
5. The executive team will address potential concerns or resistance by communicating the benefits of the 9-Box Model, addressing misconceptions, and providing support to employees throughout the process. They will also ensure that the process is transparent and objective, minimizing the potential for biases or favoritism.
6. Innovation School District will track the success of the 9-Box Model implementation by monitoring key performance indicators such as employee retention, promotions, and leadership development progress. They will also gather feedback from employees and managers to identify areas for improvement and adjust the process accordingly.
7. The 9-Box Model can be adapted to better align with the specific needs and values of Innovation School District by incorporating additional criteria relevant to the district, such as commitment to diversity and inclusion, collaboration, and community engagement.
8. To ensure the process remains transparent and objective, the district will establish clear guidelines and assessment criteria, provide training for those involved in the assessment process, and maintain open communication with employees about the purpose and goals of the 9-Box Model.
9. Measures to ensure employee confidentiality during the 9-Box Model assessment process will include restricting access to assessment results to authorized personnel, maintaining secure records, and anonymizing data when sharing it for analysis or decision-making purposes.
10. Innovation School District will communicate the implementation of the 9-Box Model and its benefits to employees through a variety of channels, such as town hall meetings, newsletters, intranet updates, and informational sessions. The district will also encourage open dialogue and feedback from employees to address any concerns and ensure a successful implementation.

Chapter 10
Intersectional Leadership

The concept of intersectional leadership is rooted in the broader idea of intersectionality, which was first introduced by legal scholar and civil rights advocate Kimberlé Crenshaw in 1989, who if you recall in chapter four, also developed the Anti-Oppression Framework. Crenshaw developed the concept of intersectionality to describe how different social categories, such as race, gender, class, and sexuality, intersect and overlap, creating unique experiences of discrimination and privilege for individuals who belong to multiple marginalized groups.

While intersectionality was initially developed within the context of legal and social theories, the concept has since been widely applied to various fields, including leadership and organizational management. Intersectional leadership builds upon the foundational ideas of intersectionality, emphasizing the importance of recognizing and addressing the multiple dimensions of identity that can influence an individual's experiences, opportunities, and challenges in the workplace.

Intersectional leadership seeks to create more inclusive, equitable, and diverse environments by considering the diverse perspectives and experiences of all individuals within an organization or community. By acknowledging and addressing the interconnected nature of various aspects of an individual's identity, intersectional leaders can work towards dismantling systemic inequalities and power dynamics, ultimately fostering a more just and inclusive organizational culture.

The Intersectional Leadership Model (ILM) is a comprehensive approach to leadership that integrates the principles of intersectionality, inclusivity, equity, and social justice. This model seeks to empower leaders to create diverse, inclusive, and equitable environments that foster a sense of belonging and empowerment for everyone.

The ILM is comprised of five key components:

1. Awareness and Education:
   - Continuously educate oneself on intersectionality and its impact on individuals and organizations.
   - Actively recognize and address one's own biases and blind spots.
   - Encourage ongoing learning and development on diversity, equity, and inclusion within the organization.

2. Empathy and Communication:
   - Foster open, respectful, and empathetic communication channels with team members.
   - Validate and acknowledge the unique experiences and perspectives of each individual.
   - Encourage active listening and empathetic engagement with diverse perspectives.

3. Inclusive Environment and Culture:
   - Create a psychologically safe and supportive environment where everyone feels valued and included.
   - Establish norms and practices that promote respect, open communication, and collaboration.
   - Implement policies and practices that support diversity, equity, and inclusion at all levels of the organization.

4. Advocacy and Action:
   - Advocate for social justice and address systemic inequalities within the organization and community.
   - Challenge the status quo and push for policies and practices that promote equity and inclusivity.
   - Hold oneself and others accountable for creating an inclusive and equitable workplace culture.

5. Collaboration and Relationship-Building:
   - Develop strong relationships with diverse stakeholders, both within and outside the organization.
   - Foster collaboration and teamwork by creating opportunities for cross-functional interactions and problem-solving.
   - Value and leverage diverse perspectives and experiences to drive innovation and success.

With implementing the Intersectional Leadership Model (ILM), leaders can work towards dismantling systemic inequalities and power dynamics, ultimately fostering a more just, inclusive, and equitable organizational culture. This model serves as a guide for leaders to navigate the complexities of intersectionality and create environments that empower all individuals, regardless of their background or identity.

The ILM also aims to address systemic inequalities and power dynamics by considering the unique challenges faced by individuals who belong to multiple marginalized or underrepresented groups. By understanding and addressing these intersecting aspects of identity, intersectional leaders can create more inclusive, equitable, and diverse environments that foster a sense of belonging and empowerment for everyone.

KEY ASPECTS OF THE ILM INCLUDE:

Awareness: Intersectional leaders are aware of the multiple dimensions of identity that can influence an individual's experiences and opportunities. They are committed to learning about and understanding the complexities of intersectionality and how it impacts the people they lead.

Empathy: Intersectional leaders show empathy and compassion towards the experiences of others, recognizing that everyone's journey is unique and shaped by various aspects of their identity.

Inclusivity: Intersectional leaders strive to create inclusive environments where everyone feels welcome, valued, and respected, regardless of their background or identity.

Advocacy: Intersectional leaders advocate for social justice and work to address systemic inequalities within their organizations and communities. They challenge the status quo and push for policies and practices that promote equity and inclusivity.

Collaboration: Intersectional leaders value collaboration and work to build strong relationships with diverse stakeholders. They understand that diverse perspectives can lead to more innovative and effective solutions.

By embracing intersectional leadership, leaders can better understand and address the unique challenges faced by individuals from diverse backgrounds, ultimately creating more inclusive and equitable organizations and communities.

Inclusive Leadership emphasizes the importance of leaders modeling inclusive behaviors and practices. Leaders who demonstrate a commitment to diversity, equity, and inclusion can help to create a workplace culture that values and supports all employees.

Intersectional leadership is a style of leadership that values and leverages the diversity of individuals and groups to create a sense of belonging and empowerment. It involves actively seeking out and valuing diverse perspectives, experiences, and ideas, and fostering an environment where everyone feels respected, valued, and heard.

Intersectional leaders recognize and appreciate the unique contributions of each individual, regardless of their background, identity, or personal characteristics. They are committed to creating a workplace culture that is diverse, equitable, and inclusive, where everyone feels welcomed and able to contribute to their fullest potential.

Intersectional leadership also involves actively challenging and dismantling systemic barriers and biases that may prevent certain individuals or groups from fully participating and contributing. It requires a willingness to engage in difficult conversations and to take action to create positive change.

Ultimately, intersectional leadership aims to create a workplace culture that values diversity, equity, and inclusion as core principles, and that leverages the power of these principles to drive innovation, growth, and success.

There are various models for intersectional leadership, but one widely recognized model is the Diversity and Inclusion (D&I) Wheel, developed by the Center for Creative Leadership. The D&I Wheel consists of three overlapping and interconnected areas of focus:

Personal Awareness: Intersectional leaders have a deep understanding of their own biases, assumptions, and values. They are aware of their own cultural background and identity, and recognize how these factors shape their perspective and behavior. In addition, they actively seek out feedback and perspectives from others to continually learn and grow.

Building Relationships: Intersectional leaders build strong, authentic relationships with people from diverse backgrounds. They are skilled at communicating across differences and creating a sense of trust and mutual respect. They also actively seek out opportunities to connect people from different backgrounds and facilitate collaboration.

Creating an Inclusive Environment: Intersectional leaders create an environment where everyone feels welcomed, respected, and valued. They promote fairness, equity, and transparency in policies and practices. They also actively seek out and respond to feedback from employees to identify and address issues related to diversity, equity, and inclusion.

VISITOR-RESIDENT FRAMEWORK

In the realm of organizational culture, the distinction between visitors and residents offers an insightful perspective on employee engagement and commitment. Visitors, akin to temporary guests, enter the workplace with minimal investment or connection to the organization, fulfilling their tasks without a strong sense of belonging or responsibility. They contribute to the environment but remain detached, seldom striving for its betterment. On the contrary, residents embody a sense of ownership and dedication to the organization. They immerse themselves in the workplace culture, nurturing familiarity and comfort within the space. As proactive stakeholders, residents continually seek ways to enhance the environment, contributing to its growth and long-term success. The distinction between visitors and residents underscores the importance of fostering a sense of belonging and commitment among employees, ultimately cultivating a thriving and sustainable organizational ecosystem.

The Visitor-Resident Engagement Framework aims to help organizations foster a sense of belonging and commitment among employees by identifying and implementing strategies that transform visitors into residents, thereby cultivating a thriving and sustainable organizational ecosystem.

Components of the Framework:

1. Identification and Assessment
   - Assess employee engagement levels within the organization.
   - Identify the characteristics and behaviors of visitors and residents among the workforce.

2. Cultural Transformation
   - Establish a strong organizational culture that promotes a sense of belonging and commitment.
   - Communicate the organization's values, mission, and vision to employees, ensuring alignment with their personal values and goals.

3. Skill Development and Growth Opportunities
   - Provide employees with opportunities for skill development, career advancement, and personal growth.
   - Implement mentorship, coaching, and training programs tailored to individual needs and aspirations.

4. Employee Recognition and Rewards
   - Recognize and reward employees for their contributions, achievements, and commitment to the organization.
   - Implement an effective performance management system that focuses on individual strengths and areas for improvement.

5. Collaboration and Team Building
   - Foster collaboration and teamwork through team-building activities, open communication channels, and opportunities for cross-functional interactions.
   - Create a psychologically safe environment that encourages employees to share ideas, provide feedback, and take risks.

6. Employee Retention and Well-being
   - Address factors that influence employee retention, such as competitive compensation, work-life balance, and job satisfaction.
   - Implement employee well-being initiatives that promote physical and mental health, as well as overall satisfaction.

7. Continuous Evaluation and Improvement
   - Regularly evaluate the effectiveness of the Visitor-Resident Engagement Framework by measuring employee engagement, commitment, and performance.
   - Implement feedback loops to continuously improve the framework and adapt to changing organizational needs and employee expectations.

By implementing the Visitor-Resident Engagement Framework, organizations can foster a culture of belonging and commitment, transforming visitors into residents who actively contribute to the organization's long-term success and sustainability.

Build Capacity with Strategy

As leaders, it's essential to embrace intersectional leadership and adopt strategies that foster a diverse, equitable, and inclusive workplace culture. These strategies will not only drive innovation and success but also create an environment where everyone feels valued and included.

To be an intersectional leader, commit to continuous education through ongoing learning about diversity, equity, and inclusion issues. Read literature, attend workshops, and engage in conversations with people from various backgrounds to gain a deeper understanding of different experiences.

Work towards creating a culture of belonging where everyone feels valued and included. Establish norms and practices that promote psychological safety, respect, and open communication. Facilitate opportunities for employees to connect and build relationships with one another.

Intentionally assemble diverse teams for job openings, striving to create teams that reflect the diversity of the wider community. Recognize the value of different perspectives and experiences, and actively seek input from all team members.

Support employees in seeking and providing feedback on their experiences and take their feedback seriously. Create a brave space for employees to voice their concerns, actively responding to the issues raised, whether through policy and practice changes or addressing factors impacting workplace culture.

Ensure that policies and practices are equitable, providing everyone with access to the resources and opportunities they need to succeed. Recognize and address systemic barriers that may hinder certain individuals or groups from fully participating and contributing.

Model desired behaviors and attitudes you want to see in others. Treat everyone with respect, listen actively, and seek out diverse perspectives. Challenge biases and discriminatory behaviors when they arise, and hold yourself and others accountable for fostering an inclusive workplace culture.

Why it Matters

Improves business outcomes: Intersectional leaders create a work environment where all employees feel valued, respected, and empowered to contribute their best work. This leads to increased engagement, productivity, and innovation, which ultimately translates into better business outcomes.

Promotes diversity and equity: Intersectional leaders recognize and value the diverse experiences and perspectives of their team members. By creating a culture of inclusion, they attract and retain a diverse workforce, which enhances creativity and problem-solving abilities.

They also work to promote equity by dismantling systemic barriers that may prevent certain individuals or groups from fully participating and contributing.

Fosters a positive work culture: Intersectional leadership creates a positive work culture where everyone feels supported and valued. This leads to higher employee morale, job satisfaction, and retention.

Builds brand reputation: Intersectional leaders who prioritize diversity and equity are viewed positively by customers, investors, and the wider community. This can enhance the organization's brand reputation and increase customer loyalty.

Promotes social responsibility: Intersectional leaders recognize their responsibility to promote equity and social justice, and take action to create positive change. They leverage their position of influence to advocate for underrepresented groups, and drive progress towards a more equitable and inclusive society.

Intersectional leadership is essential for creating a workplace culture that values and leverages diversity, promotes equity and inclusion, and drives innovation and success. By prioritizing intersectional leadership practices, leaders can create a better workplace for their employees and a stronger business for their organization.

Integration of Strategies

Intersectional leadership is a crucial element in building resilient workforces, as it acknowledges and addresses various dimensions of diversity, equity, and inclusion. By applying different frameworks and concepts, intersectional leaders create an environment where employees feel valued, supported, and empowered.

8. Equity-Based Hiring: Implement hiring practices that promote equity and diversity, such as blind resume review and targeted outreach to underrepresented groups, to build a diverse and inclusive workforce.
1. Symbolic Interaction: Foster open communication and active listening in the workplace, and create opportunities for collaborative

problem-solving, thus encouraging shared meaning and interaction among employees.

2. Affinity Grouping: Support the establishment of spaces for individuals with shared identities or experiences to come together, fostering resilience in the face of discrimination and other challenges.

3. Equity & Justice: Emphasize the importance of promoting equity and justice in the workplace by addressing discrimination, stereotypes, and their impact on individuals' performance and well-being.

4. Feminist Framework: Advocate for gender equity and create a workplace culture that supports all genders, acknowledging the impact of gender inequality and discrimination on the work environment.

5. Stereotype Threat: Recognize the impact of negative stereotypes on individual performance and well-being, and create a supportive and inclusive workplace culture for all employees.

6. Ecosystem of Racism: Address racism and other forms of discrimination at a systemic level by implementing policies and practices that promote equity and justice, recognizing that these issues can be deeply embedded in social systems and structures.

7. Cybernetics: Employ feedback and self-correction mechanisms in the workplace, promoting continuous learning and improvement to create effective and adaptable systems.

8. Succession Planning: Develop a plan for identifying and developing the next generation of leaders within the organization, providing opportunities for training, development, mentorship, and support.

Embrace the power of intersectional leadership and unlock your organization's true potential! By integrating these transformative frameworks and strategies into your leadership style, you can champion resilience, celebrate diversity, and foster an inclusive environment that empowers every team member.

Take time to learn about issues related to intersectionality, including your own biases and blind spots. This involves reading literature, attending workshops, and engaging in conversations with people from different backgrounds to gain a deeper understanding of the experiences of others.

Take the time to get to know your team members as individuals. Ask about their experiences, interests, and perspectives. Be open to learning from them, and create opportunities for them to connect with one another and build relationships. Commit to seeing them before seeing the work.

Establish norms and practices that promote psychological safety, respect, and open communication. Foster an environment where everyone feels valued and included. Encourage employees to share their opinions and ideas, and make sure everyone has a chance to be heard. Be intentional about creating a team that reflects the diversity of the wider community, and recognize the value of different perspectives and experiences.

Encourage employees to provide feedback on their experiences, and take this feedback seriously. Create a brave space for employees to share their concerns, and actively respond to concerns that are raised. This can involve making changes to policies and practices, or addressing issues that are impacting the workplace culture.

Model the behaviors and attitudes you want to see in others. Treat everyone with respect, listen actively, and seek out diverse perspectives. Challenge biases and discriminatory behaviors when they arise, and hold yourself and others accountable for creating an inclusive workplace culture.

By taking these steps you can build resilience in a workplace culture that values and leverages diversity, promotes equity and inclusion, and drives innovation and success. It's important to remember that intersectional leadership is an ongoing process that requires continuous learning, reflection, and action. Unite your workforce under a shared vision and together you'll drive unparalleled success.

Don't wait – seize the opportunity to make a difference and be the change you wish to see in your workplace. Your journey as an inspiring, intersectional leader starts now!

Intersectional Leadership

INTERSECTIONAL LEADERSHIP: BUILDING RESILIENT WORKFORCES

Key Questions

How does intersectional leadership differ from traditional leadership styles?

Intersectional leadership differs from traditional leadership styles in that it specifically acknowledges and addresses the interconnected nature of various aspects of an individual's identity, such as race, gender, class, sexual orientation, disability, and ethnicity, and how these factors influence their experiences and opportunities. Traditional leadership styles may not take these intersecting aspects of identity into account, which can lead to a less inclusive and equitable environment.

Why is empathy important in intersectional leadership?

Empathy is important in intersectional leadership because it allows leaders to understand and relate to the unique experiences and challenges faced by individuals from diverse backgrounds. By showing empathy and compassion, intersectional leaders demonstrate that they value and respect each person's journey, fostering an environment where everyone feels supported and included.

How can intersectional leaders create a more inclusive environment in their organizations?

Intersectional leaders can create a more inclusive environment by promoting awareness of intersectionality, showing empathy towards diverse experiences, fostering inclusivity, advocating for social justice, and collaborating with diverse stakeholders. By actively addressing systemic inequalities and power dynamics, intersectional leaders can create a workplace culture that values diversity, equity, and inclusion.

What are the benefits of intersectional leadership for organizations and communities?

The benefits of intersectional leadership for organizations and communities include increased innovation and creativity, enhanced problem-solving abilities, improved employee satisfaction and retention, and a more inclusive and equitable environment. By valuing and leveraging the diversity of individuals and groups, intersectional leadership fosters a sense of belonging and empowerment that can lead to greater success and growth.

How can leaders incorporate intersectional leadership principles into their existing leadership styles?

Leaders can incorporate intersectional leadership principles into their existing leadership styles by becoming aware of the multiple dimensions of identity that influence an individual's experiences and opportunities, demonstrating empathy and compassion towards diverse experiences, fostering inclusivity, advocating for social justice, and collaborating with diverse stakeholders. By embracing these principles, leaders can create more inclusive, equitable, and diverse environments that promote a sense of belonging and empowerment for everyone.

How does intersectional leadership help in addressing systemic inequalities and power dynamics?

Intersectional leadership helps in addressing systemic inequalities and power dynamics by considering the unique challenges faced by individuals who belong to multiple marginalized or underrepresented groups. By understanding and addressing these intersecting aspects of identity, intersectional leaders can create more inclusive, equitable, and diverse environments that foster a sense of belonging and empowerment for everyone, ultimately challenging and dismantling systemic barriers and biases.

What role does personal awareness play in intersectional leadership?

Personal awareness plays a critical role in intersectional leadership, as it involves understanding one's own biases, assumptions, and values, as well as recognizing how one's cultural background and identity shape perspectives and behaviors. By actively seeking feedback and perspectives from others, intersectional leaders can continually learn and grow, becoming more effective in leading diverse teams and creating inclusive environments.

Key Questions (cont.)

How can intersectional leaders promote equity in their organizations?

Intersectional leaders can promote equity in their organizations by ensuring that policies and practices are fair and equitable, and that everyone has access to the resources and opportunities they need to succeed. They can also recognize and address systemic barriers that may be preventing certain individuals or groups from fully participating and contributing. This may involve making changes to policies and practices, or addressing issues that impact the workplace culture.

In what ways can intersectional leadership drive innovation and success in the workplace?

Intersectional leadership can drive innovation and success in the workplace by fostering an environment where diverse perspectives, experiences, and ideas are valued and leveraged. By creating a culture that supports and encourages diverse viewpoints and collaboration, intersectional leaders can facilitate the development of more innovative and effective solutions to challenges, ultimately leading to greater success and growth for the organization.

How can leaders ensure that their intersectional leadership approach is effective and impactful?

Leaders can ensure that their intersectional leadership approach is effective and impactful by continuously educating themselves on issues related to diversity, equity, and inclusion, creating a culture of belonging, building diverse teams, encouraging and listening to feedback, promoting equity, and leading by example. By adopting these strategies and being committed to creating an inclusive workplace culture, leaders can make a positive impact on their organizations and the individuals within them.

Practice 10.1

A mid-sized technology company has recently experienced rapid growth and is looking to expand its workforce. The company's leadership team, led by the CEO, Sarah, recognizes the importance of intersectional leadership in creating a diverse and inclusive workplace. The team is now faced with the challenge of incorporating intersectional leadership practices in their recruitment and retention strategies.

1. What steps can Sarah and the leadership team take to educate themselves on intersectional leadership and the importance of diversity, equity, and inclusion in the workplace?

2. How can the company's recruitment process be modified to attract a diverse pool of candidates and ensure that intersectional leadership principles are incorporated into the hiring process?

3. What strategies can Sarah and the leadership team implement to create a culture of belonging and inclusivity within the company, both for existing employees and new hires?

4. How can the company's leadership team ensure that they are actively listening to feedback from employees, particularly those from underrepresented groups, and address any concerns or challenges that are raised?

5. What resources or development opportunities can the company provide to help employees from diverse backgrounds grow their skills and prepare for leadership roles within the organization?

6. How can Sarah and the leadership team demonstrate their commitment to intersectional leadership and set a positive example for the rest of the company?

7. How can the company measure the success of their intersectional leadership initiatives and continuously improve their diversity, equity, and inclusion efforts?

Practice 10.2

Group Activity

Transforming Visitors to Residents

Objective:

To facilitate the understanding and implementation of the Visitor-Resident Engagement Framework, promoting a sense of belonging, commitment, and collaboration among employees.

Duration 90 minutes

Materials

- Flipchart or whiteboard
- Markers
- Sticky notes
- Pens or pencils
- Handout with the Visitor-Resident Engagement Framework

Instructions

1. Introduction: Begin by presenting the concept of the Visitor-Resident Engagement Framework to the participants. Explain the distinction between visitors and residents, and the importance of fostering a sense of belonging and commitment among employees to create a thriving and sustainable organizational ecosystem.

2. Group Formation: Divide participants into groups of 4-6 people. Encourage diversity within each group by mixing people from different departments, backgrounds, or levels of experience.

3. Framework Exploration: Provide each group with a handout detailing the Visitor-Resident Engagement Framework. Instruct the groups to discuss and analyze the components of the framework, focusing on how they can be implemented within their organization.

4. Action Planning: Ask each group to identify one or two components of the framework that they believe are particularly relevant or have the most significant impact on their organization. Instruct the groups to create an action plan for implementing these components,

outlining specific steps, resources needed, and potential challenges.

5. Presentations: Invite a representative from each group to present their action plan to the entire group. Allocate 5-7 minutes for each presentation, allowing time for questions and feedback from the other participants.

6. Collective Insights: After all presentations, facilitate a group discussion on the insights and ideas shared by each group. Encourage participants to consider common themes, challenges, and opportunities for collaboration across the organization.

7. Next Steps: Conclude the activity by discussing possible next steps for implementing the action plans within the organization. Encourage participants to take ownership of their plans and collaborate with their colleagues to transform visitors into residents.

The Transforming Visitors to Residents activity promotes collaboration, understanding, and the implementation of the Visitor-Resident Engagement Framework among team members. It enables participants to take an active role in fostering a sense of belonging and commitment within their organization, ultimately contributing to its long-term success and sustainability.

Practice 10.3

Group Activity
Integration of Strategies Debrief

Objective:
To facilitate reflection and discussion on the integration of intersectional leadership strategies to build a resilient and diverse workforce.

Duration 45 minutes

Materials
- Whiteboard or flipchart
- Markers
- Sticky notes (optional)

Instructions

1. Divide participants into small groups (4-6 people per group).

2. Ask each group to discuss their experiences with implementing or observing the intersectional leadership strategies mentioned in the prompt. They should reflect on the following questions:

   - What strategies have been effective in your organization or workplace?
   - What challenges have you faced in implementing these strategies?
   - How have these strategies impacted your organization's culture, diversity, and overall performance?

3. After 15-20 minutes of discussion, bring the groups back together and ask a representative from each group to share their key takeaways and insights with the larger group.

4. Write these key takeaways on the whiteboard or flipchart, creating a visual representation of the shared experiences and learnings.

5. Facilitate a whole-group discussion on the following topics:

   - Identify any common themes or patterns in the experiences shared.

- Discuss potential solutions or strategies to overcome the challenges faced in implementing intersectional leadership practices.
- Share any additional resources or support needed for successful implementation and ongoing improvement.
6. Conclude the activity by summarizing the key insights and learnings, and encourage participants to commit to implementing one or more of the discussed strategies in their workplace.

This debrief protocol activity will help participants reflect on their experiences with intersectional leadership strategies, identify areas for improvement, and commit to taking action to foster a more inclusive and resilient workplace.

Intersectional Leadership: Building Resilient Workforces

Answer Key 10.1

1. Steps for Sarah and the leadership team to educate themselves on intersectional leadership and the importance of diversity, equity, and inclusion in the workplace:
   - ☐ Read literature and research on intersectionality, diversity, and inclusion.
   - ☐ Attend workshops, conferences, and seminars on these topics.
   - ☐ Engage in conversations with diverse groups and individuals.
   - ☐ Seek mentorship or coaching from experienced leaders in this area.
   - ☐ Invite guest speakers or trainers to address the leadership team on intersectional leadership.

2. Modifying the company's recruitment process to attract diverse candidates and incorporate intersectional leadership principles:
   - ☐ Revise job postings to use inclusive language and highlight diversity and inclusion commitments.
   - ☐ Expand recruitment efforts to target diverse talent pools, such as partnering with minority-serving organizations.
   - ☐ Implement blind recruitment practices to reduce unconscious bias.
   - ☐ Train hiring managers on intersectional leadership and inclusive interviewing techniques.
   - ☐ Include diverse interview panel members to ensure multiple perspectives are considered during the hiring process.

3. Strategies for creating a culture of belonging and inclusivity within the company:
   - ☐ Develop and communicate clear diversity, equity, and inclusion policies and goals.
   - ☐ Create employee resource groups for underrepresented employees to foster connections and support.
   - ☐ Implement regular diversity and inclusion training for all employees.
   - ☐ Encourage open communication and collaboration among team members.
   - ☐ Celebrate diverse perspectives and create opportunities for employees to share their experiences and ideas.

4. Ensuring active listening to feedback from employees and addressing concerns or challenges:
   - ☐ Conduct regular employee surveys to gather feedback on diversity, equity, and inclusion efforts.
   - ☐ Organize town hall meetings or focus groups to facilitate open conversations.
   - ☐ Implement an anonymous feedback system for employees to share concerns without fear of retaliation.
   - ☐ Establish clear processes for addressing employee concerns and provide regular updates on actions taken.

5. Resources or development opportunities to help diverse employees grow their skills and prepare for leadership roles:
   - ☐ Offer mentorship or sponsorship programs to support career growth.
   - ☐ Provide training and development programs focused on building leadership skills.
   - ☐ Offer opportunities for employees to participate in cross-functional projects to gain new experiences.
   - ☐ Encourage and support attendance at conferences or workshops related to their areas of interest or expertise.
6. Demonstrating commitment to intersectional leadership and setting a positive example:
   - ☐ Publicly share the company's diversity, equity, and inclusion goals and progress.
   - ☐ Regularly communicate the importance of intersectional leadership to employees.
   - ☐ Model inclusive behaviors, such as actively seeking diverse perspectives and challenging biases.
   - ☐ Hold leaders accountable for promoting diversity, equity, and inclusion within their teams.
7. Measuring the success of intersectional leadership initiatives and improving diversity, equity, and inclusion efforts:
   - ☐ Track metrics related to diversity, such as the demographic makeup of the workforce and leadership.
   - ☐ Monitor employee engagement and satisfaction levels, particularly among underrepresented groups.
   - ☐ Assess the success of specific diversity, equity, and inclusion initiatives through surveys, focus groups, or interviews.
   - ☐ Regularly review and adjust policies, practices, and goals based on the collected data and feedback.

REFERENCES

Chapter 1:

Tajfel, H., & Turner, J. C. (1979). An integrative theory of intergroup conflict. In W. G. Austin & S. Worchel (Eds.), The social psychology of intergroup relations (pp. 33-47). Brooks/Cole.

Chapter 2:

Mead, G. H. (1934). Mind, self, and society. University of Chicago Press.

Cooley, C. H. (1902). Human nature and the social order. Charles Scribner's Sons.

Chapter 3:

Masten, A. S. (2014). Ordinary magic: Resilience in development. Guilford Publications.

Chapter 4:

Crenshaw, K. (1989). Demarginalizing the intersection of race and sex: A black feminist critique of antidiscrimination doctrine, feminist theory, and antiracist politics. University of Chicago Legal Forum, 1(8), 139-167.

Adams, M., Bell, L. A., & Griffin, P. (2007). Teaching for diversity and social justice. Routledge.

Chapter 5:

Wollstonecraft, M. (1792). A vindication of the rights of woman. J. Johnson.

Fortune. (2023). Fortune 500 list. Retrieved from https://fortune.com/fortune500/2023/search/

Zippia. (2022). These states have the most female superintendents. Retrieved from https://www.zippia.com/advice/female-school-superintendents-by-state/

Grant Thornton. (2022). Women in business: Beyond policy to progress. Retrieved from https://www.grantthornton.global/globalassets/1.-member-firms/global/women-in-business/2022/reports/ibt-2022-report.pdf

U.S. Bureau of Labor Statistics. (2021). Women in the labor force: A databook. Retrieved from https://www.bls.gov/opub/reports/womens-databook/2021/home.htm

Inter-Parliamentary Union. (2022). Women in national parliaments. Retrieved from https://data.ipu.org/content/women-in-national-parliaments

Catalyst. (2023). Women CEOs of the S&P 500. Retrieved from https://www.catalyst.org/research/women-ceos-of-the-sp-500/

Chapter 6:

Steele, C. M., & Aronson, J. (1995). Stereotype threat and the intellectual test performance of African Americans. Journal of Personality and Social Psychology, 69(5), 797-811.

Chapter 7:

Bronfenbrenner, U. (1979). The ecology of human development. Harvard University Press.

Chapter 8:

Wiener, N. (1948). Cybernetics: Or control and communication in the animal and the machine. MIT Press.

Chapter 9:

Rasiel, E. M., & Friga, P. N. (2001). The McKinsey mind: Understanding and implementing the problem-solving tools and management techniques of the world's top strategic consulting firm. McGraw-Hill.

Chapter 10:

Crenshaw, K. (1989). Demarginalizing the intersection of race and sex: A black feminist critique of antidiscrimination doctrine, feminist theory, and antiracist politics. University of Chicago Legal Forum, 1(8), 139-167.

Hannum, K. M., Martineau, J. W., & Reinelt, C. (2007). The handbook of leadership development evaluation. Center for Creative Leadership

Made in the USA
Monee, IL
06 October 2023